Introduction: Developing Quality RE

Wouldn't it be good ... ?

... **if** pupils and parents were pleasantly surprised by their first experience of religious education (RE), setting aside negative views of the subject, and finding it imaginative, engaging, creative, challenging and relevant?

... **if** it was a favourite lesson with pupils, so that when they knew an RE lesson was coming up they asked, 'What will we do this time?'

... **if** work in RE was making a special contribution to their skills in language, self-expression, co-operation and understanding?

... **if** RE was enabling them to develop attitudes of confidence and thoughtfulness about their own beliefs, and tolerance and respect towards other people?

... **if** children found space in RE to explore their own beliefs, and to spend some time building up understanding of different world religions?

... **if** they had the chance to think about their own experiences of life, in the light of some of the treasures of faith?

... **if** they found in their RE ways to respond to the experiences of life, both happy and sad, that helped them to be more fully human?

... **if** Ofsted inspectors noticed that RE was making a significant contribution to the whole school's aims, and to the spiritual and moral development of all pupils?

... **if** at the end of their time at your school, children made the kind of comments quoted in the box above?

'RE gave me the chance to ask the questions that had always puzzled me about God.'

'I really enjoyed learning not just about Christianity (my own religion) but other religions. Living in a multicultural society, it's important to understand what goes on around you. I think RE definitely makes you a more thoughtful person.'

'I have been given an insight into many other cultures and beliefs. The most satisfying aspect is that RE is helping me to mature in my attitude to life. RE enables me to develop my own concepts and views, and it's a mind-expanding experience.'

'I have found it good to learn from religions about how believers cope with everyday life.'

These comments come from pupils at the end of their RE courses, but quality RE begins with the very early years. **This book aims to provide teachers with information and practical ideas that will enable them to plan more effective, inspiring and challenging RE across the 4–19 age range.**

RE can be a difficult subject to teach because it deals with truth claims in an uncertain field and its area of enquiry is vast. Some teachers are uncertain about the contribution RE can make to pupils' learning, and others find it a hard subject to teach because of their own experience of religion and life. Those with strong religious convictions of their own need to find an educational approach to RE; the same applies to the teacher who is an atheist or an agnostic. Pupils often come to RE with negative attitudes, picked up from a secular society in which religion can be marginalised, and parents sometimes may question the aims that a school is pursuing.

These problems should not obscure the rich potential of the subject to contribute to the human development of young people. High-quality religious education can draw upon some of the great religions of the world and enable pupils to explore the questions of meaning that life throws up in the light of the insights of faith. RE can also enable young people to carry forward their own personal search for what is true, and what is good. **We hope this book will enable teachers who use it to build this kind of RE.**

Section 1 RE Subject Leadership

Providing a framework for quality RE

What is the Framework and who produced it?

In October 2004 the Qualifications and Curriculum Authority (QCA, England) published a non-statutory National Framework for Religious Education. It was produced to act as a support to those with responsibility for the provision and quality of RE in maintained schools. It seeks to support them through offering a clear and shared understanding of the knowledge and skills children and young people should have opportunity to develop through their RE entitlement and experience and it provides a focus for agreeing standards of attainment across the different phases.

Do I now have to follow the Framework?

No. The legal situation of delivering RE based on the locally agreed syllabus (or trust deeds / faith community guidelines) has not changed (see page 6).

What's its purpose then?

The Framework sets out a structure for Agreed Syllabus Conferences (and for faith communities) to select and use to determine what pupils should be taught in RE. **It is neither a syllabus, nor a scheme of work, and schools should not attempt to use it as such**.

Many Agreed Syllabus Conferences, when their syllabus is reviewed (on a five-yearly cycle), are using the Framework to inform developments. Within the next few years it is highly likely that many syllabuses will reflect aspects of the Framework.

A number of publishers are providing RE material which takes into consideration the expectations of the Framework. Schools still need to ensure that this material meets the requirements of their current locally agreed syllabus (trust deeds / faith community guidelines).

What about the QCA units of work?

As part of its development work for Religious Education the QCA has also reviewed its non-statutory units of work, to take Framework considerations on board. Some new sample units of work (two for the Foundation Stage, two for Key Stage 1, four for Key Stage 2 and three for Key Stage 3) are available on the QCA's website: www.qca.org.uk.

Whilst there is useful material here **schools need to ensure that they relate what they do to their current locally agreed syllabus (trust deeds / faith community guidelines)**.

The Framework: structure

The Framework provides an overview of what should be studied in RE from the ages of 3 to 19, organised in three sections:

Foundation Stage (ages 3–5) sets out expectations of what children should learn to meet the Early Learning Goals. The Framework describes how RE can contribute to these goals and provides examples of RE-related activities for this age group.

Key Stages 1 to 3 (ages 5–14) follows the same format as the National Curriculum programmes of study with sections on:

- **knowledge, skills and understanding** – identifying the key aspects of learning in RE (learning about and learning from religion)

- **breadth of study** – the knowledge, skills and understanding are developed through the breadth of study which has three elements:

  - religions and beliefs

  - themes

  - experiences and opportunities.

Ages 14–19. The Framework sets out an entitlement to study Religious Education in a progressed way 14–16 and 16–19, and for pupils to have their learning accredited.

Which religions do I have to teach?

An agreed syllabus must reflect the fact that 'the religious traditions in Great Britain are in the main Christian, while taking account of the teaching and practices of other principal religions represented in Great Britain' (s375 (3) Education Act 1996 – see p.9). How this is achieved varies slightly across syllabuses: check what yours requires. The other principal religions have been taken to be: Buddhism, Hinduism, Islam, Judaism and Sikhism.

The Framework suggests for Key Stages 1 to 3 that Christianity and the other principal religions are focused on and a religion with a significant local presence or secular worldviews (where appropriate) could also form part of the programme of study.

The Framework has 'themes' – should we teach thematically?

No. Your locally agreed syllabus/faith community guidelines will give you a steer on how to organise your teaching. Many suggest, as appropriate to the ages and abilities of your pupils, a mixture of:

- **A thematic approach** which emphasises concepts across and between religions and often relates directly to pupils' own experiences. This approach can easily be incorporated into a cross-curricular approach.

- **A systematic approach** which emphasises the content of the religion being studied and can lead to a coherent understanding of what it means to belong to a particular religion. It also makes it easier to quantify the time given to each principal religion and therefore makes it easier to show the balance achieved between different religions.

- **An issues-based approach** which combines elements of both the thematic and systematic – developing conceptual understanding through themes, but also giving an overview of each religion studied. It is based on fundamental questions of human existence and is therefore of relevance to the individual in his or her personal development.

The Framework: levels

The level descriptions provide key indicators of the expectations for attainment in RE progressed from level 1 through to level 8 and beyond to Exceptional Performance.

Levels in your locally agreed syllabus /faith community guidelines provide a useful focus for both assessment for learning and for summative assessment (see pp.25–34) as well as a useful check on the quality of task setting.

- Do the activities allow for pupils to achieve the appropriate level?

- What needs to happen to support those working towards it or those working beyond it?

Progressed skills can be identified through the levels. For example:

- **Level 1**: recognise and name, recall, talk about

- **Level 2**: use religious words, awareness of similarities, retell and suggest meaning, identify

- **Level 3**: describe, recognise similarities and differences, making links, ask questions, etc.

Useful web links

- **The QCA's non-statutory Framework** for RE can be downloaded from www. qca.org.uk.

- **The non-statutory units of work** are available on the QCA site: www.qca.org.uk.

Thematic	Systematic	Issues-based
Special places	Christianity	Is there a God?
Festivals	• in the locality	Is the Bible true?
Family and friends	• worship	Why is there suffering?
Creation	• belonging	What do I believe?

The role of the subject leader

A pivotal role

The role of the subject leader is a pivotal one in both primary and secondary schools. The following pages of this handbook develop some of the key areas that any subject leader needs to be aware of and to plan to develop. Further guidance can be found in the three publications indicated below:

National Standards for Subject Leaders (1998)

In this non-statutory document the Teacher Training Agency (now the Training and Development Agency) outlined the nature of the role of the subject leader. It identified five areas:

- core purpose of the subject leader
- key outcomes of subject leadership
- professional knowledge and understanding
- skills and attributes
- key areas of subject leadership.

During 2007 there will be a review of subject leader standards in the context of a review of leadership standards. The 1998 guidance remains appropriate until replaced.

Secondary National Strategy (2002)

'Securing improvement: the role of the subject leader' (DfES 0102 /2002) makes it clear that the work of the subject leader is vital, and that the subject leaders are the key contact between the Strategy and the classroom teachers. The booklet identifies three roles and indicates what each involves:

- judging standards
- evaluating teaching and learning
- leading sustainable improvement.

Primary National Strategy (2003)

The Primary Strategy materials make clear statements about the role of 'curriculum co-ordinators', which is relevant to RE. For example, it makes it clear that grouping subjects under a theme is most effective when 'curriculum co-ordinators ensured **progression within each subject was secure** within the long-term planning at each key stage ... The rigour with which each subject was planned [was] underpinned by objectives ... [and] was providing pupils with the broad curriculum to which they were entitled.'

Source: Designing Opportunities for Learning, *DfES 0520 – 2004 G.*

Core purpose

The subject leader:

- **provides professional leadership** for the subject to secure high-quality teaching, effective use of resources and improved standards of learning and achievement for all pupils.

- **provides leadership and direction for the subject and ensures it is managed and organised to meet the aims and objectives** of the school and the subject. While the headteacher and governors carry overall responsibility for school improvement, a subject leader has responsibility for securing high standards of teaching and learning in the subject as well as playing a major role in the development of school policy and practice. Throughout their work, subject leaders ensure that practices improve the quality of education provided, meet the needs and aspirations of all pupils and raise standards of achievement in the school.

- **plays a key role in supporting, guiding and motivating teachers of the subject, and other adults.** Subject leaders evaluate the effectiveness of teaching and learning, the subject curriculum and progress towards targets for pupils and staff to inform future priorities and targets for the subject.

- **identifies needs in their own subject and recognises that these must be considered in relation to the overall needs of the school.** It is important that a subject leader has an understanding of how the subject contributes to school priorities and to the overall education and achievement of all pupils.

Source: National Standards for Subject Leaders, *TTA (1998).*

Self-evaluation in Religious Education

A toolkit for subject leaders (2005)

The 2005 Ofsted inspection framework emphasises schools' own procedures for self-evaluation (see: *A New Relationship with Schools*, Ofsted 2004). **How can RE subject leaders ensure that RE adds successfully to a pupil's educational experience?**

Self-Evaluation in Religious Education: a toolkit for subject leaders (AREIAC 2005) is a document designed to support primary, secondary and special schools, where a locally agreed syllabus is followed. Page 6 of the toolkit states that it **aims to**:

- **provide** guidance on finding out how well pupils are doing in RE

- **focus** on the quality of teaching pupils receive and the opportunities they are given to develop spiritually, morally, socially and culturally

- **support** teachers in evaluating their own practice, enabling them to demonstrate that pupils are challenged in RE in ways that develop their thinking and their character

- **focus** on the role that subject leaders play in ensuring that RE adds successfully to a pupil's educational experience

- **provide** a mechanism for the RE subject leader to contribute to the school's self-evaluation form (SEF), including an assessment of the extent to which the school meets all statutory requirements regarding the subject

- **promote** the good things happening in RE, helping to draw the attention of senior managers, governors and parents to strengths in learning and teaching in RE

- **enable** the identification of areas of weakness, which may be identified for action on the school improvement plans

- **enable** subject leaders to respond to any request from the local authority's Standing Advisory Council on RE (SACRE) for information on standards in RE

- **provide** examples of evidence which may be compiled to demonstrate the effectiveness of RE in the school, completed examples and a blank template

- **provide** a measure of reassurance in highlighting strengths already in place, some pointers as to what priorities for development should be, and a little **inspiration to reach for overall excellence in RE.**

Statutory inspection of denominational schools

Section 48 denominational inspections are also part of life for voluntary aided and voluntary controlled schools. Just like Ofsted, this process relies heavily on the school's own evaluation of its performance and priorities based on the school's aims and purposes laid out in its trust deeds/ articles of government.

The inspection process focuses on how the school expresses its ethos and values derived from its faith-based foundation, including, for voluntary aided schools, addressing RE.

If you are subject leader for RE in a voluntary aided church school, take advice from your diocese about the self-evaluation tools which have been developed to aid such self-evaluation.

Useful weblinks

- **Toolkit for RE:** http://betterre.reonline.org.uk/lead_manage/toolkit.php

- *A New Relationship with Schools* **(Ofsted 2004) PP/ D16/(5585)/0604/22:** www.ofsted.gov.uk

- **National Society:** www.natsoc.org.uk

- **Catholic Education Service:** www.cesew.org.uk/index.asp?id=1

Law and RE

Does this concern me?

Yes. RE takes place within the context of both legislation and guidance – it is important not to confuse the two.

Legislation[1] is contained in the 2002 Education Act which for England forms the statutory basis for the planning and delivery of RE. The 1996 and 1998 Education Acts also contain relevant sections. The legal document that most directly impacts on the majority of schools is the locally agreed syllabus (or faith community guidelines).

Non-statutory guidance comes in different forms, e.g. Circular 1/94 (DfES), QCA's non-statutory National Framework and units of work.

'The law in England and Wales makes provision for all pupils in community schools to receive a religious education that has been agreed between different religious communities, the local authority and the teachers.

This legal framework has enabled us to develop over many years RE which makes it possible for all pupils to know their own roots and to respect the roots of others. These respectful possibilities are the envy of the world in some ways, as the steady stream of visitors from other countries to look at our RE shows.'

John Keast, RE Consultant

RE actively promotes the values of truth, justice, respect for all and care of the environment. It places specific emphasis on pupils valuing themselves and others, the role of family and the community in religious belief and activity, the celebration of diversity in society through understanding similarities and differences, and human stewardship of the earth.

Religious education also recognises the changing nature of society, including changes in religious practice and expression and the influence of religion, in the local, national and global community.

Source: QCA website, www.qca.org.uk.

What does legislation require?

1 RE is an **entitlement** for all registered pupils on the school roll (including reception and school sixth form), unless they have been withdrawn from the whole or part of the RE curriculum by their parent(s). The **right to withdraw** was first granted when religious education was actually religious instruction and carried with it connotations of induction into the Christian faith.[2] Circular 1/94 states that agreed syllabuses should not be designed to convert pupils or to urge a particular religion or religious beliefs on them (paragraph 32).

2 In **community, voluntary controlled**[3] and **foundation** schools (non-religious character), RE is delivered in accordance with the locally agreed syllabus. In **voluntary aided**[4] and **foundation** schools with a religious character, RE is delivered in accordance with the school's trust deeds, which generally means following their faith community guidelines. In **academies** RE is delivered in accordance with its articles of government. **Special schools** need to deliver RE (usually in accordance with their locally agreed syllabus) 'as far as is practicable'.

3 **Agreed syllabuses** vary in presentation, style and content, but since the publication of the QCA's non-statutory Framework more commonality is developing. All have to ensure that RE content reflects the fact that the main religious traditions

'Faith plays a key role in everyone's life. Everyone has faith in God, animals, a person, and so on. RE lessons are very, very informative and also enjoyable! The reason I say this is because I like the way we're taught and the situations we talk about are relevant in contemporary society. It's a subject that is appealing and informative - it helps you think about the present situation, you tend to hear other people's views and see what you think! It's a brilliant subject.'

Female. Sikh, aged 17, from the 'Listening to young people talking' database, www.natre.org.uk.

of Britain are Christian, whilst taking account of the other principal religions represented in Great Britain.[5] Two aspects common to most agreed syllabuses are: 'learning about' and 'learning from' religion.

Many agreed syllabuses have been drawn up on the expectation of **5 per cent of curriculum time** being given to RE (approximately one hour per week).[6] As agreed syllabuses are reviewed, many are taking on board aspects of the recommendations of the non-statutory National Framework for RE (QCA, 2004).[7]

4 **It is important not to confuse legislation regarding RE with that of collective worship** (in England there should be daily acts of worship, a majority of which should be 'wholly or mainly of a Christian nature' and should take account of the ages and backgrounds of the pupils involved. In Scotland a 'regular' act of 'religious observance' is required). The two have obvious areas of overlap and commonality, and can be mutually supportive of each other, but they are not the same in law.

What are the implications at school level?

- You must be familiar with and **use the correct syllabus** for your type of school, informing your headteacher/governors as to requirements appropriately.

- Knowing legislation can 'strengthen your hand' when you feel that RE is not being taken seriously enough. In order to do this you need to **be clear about the difference between legislation and guidance**.

- The agreed syllabus is **reviewed at least every five years**. It is good to consider your subject area/departmental improvement plan cycle bearing in mind when the agreed syllabus is going to be reviewed. This means that you would not be doing a lot of development work in the last six months before a revised syllabus is published (unless absolutely necessary) only to have to re-look at it to ensure it still meets statutory requirements.

Notes

1 Outlined on these pages is information for **England**, some of which applies in a similar way to other parts of the UK.

   In **Scotland** the Religious and Moral Education Guidelines (1992) provide a framework for curriculum development. At the time of going to print, discussion has taken place about reviewing these but no firm decision taken.

   In **Wales** a curriculum review which includes RE is in place for 2008.

   In **Northern Ireland** the Core Syllabus determines RE content (for all grant-aided schools). It acts as a basis from which schools can build a programme to suit their particular needs.

2 The **right of withdrawal** was enshrined in law in 1944. It applies to all types of schools, even those with a religious foundation. Teachers have the right to withdraw from teaching RE.

3 In **voluntary controlled schools**, parents can require RE to be delivered according to the trust deeds rather than with a locally agreed syllabus.

4 In **voluntary aided schools** parents can request delivery of RE in accordance with the locally agreed syllabus if there is no school delivering it that their child(ren) could reasonably be expected to attend.

5 **Regarded as** Buddhism, Hinduism, Islam, Judaism, Sikhism, in Circular 1/94.

6 If significantly less than **5 per cent of curriculum time** is given, then legal requirements cannot be met.

7 See pp. 2–3.

Team-building for better RE: teachers with other specialisms

Context

A major challenge for the subject co-ordinator in **primary schools** today is that of enabling colleagues with other specialisms and priorities to do a good job efficiently, with enthusiasm and integrity. Similarly, in **secondary schools**, the head of RE often leads a team of colleagues with other specialisms. In RE, perhaps more than in other subjects, this can be compounded by the different approaches to the subject among a staff team.

Some teachers have a great commitment to and interest in teaching their own faith, but not other faiths. Some teachers question the place of RE in the curriculum, often because they misunderstand the educational rationale for the subject, sometimes because they felt indoctrinated through their own experience of RE. Some teachers may exercise their right to opt out of RE teaching on conscientious grounds.

In every case, the priorities of teachers are so many that RE will not be top of the list often or for long. This is quite reasonable, and it means that when the subject is considered, once a term at a staff meeting, or through an annual CPD opportunity, the quality of input needs to be good, and the agenda needs to move forward, rather than chewing over old questions.

The issue of confidence is perhaps the most crucial. Many excellent teachers, who are able, with a little work, to do their RE really well, feel so lacking in confidence in a subject where many different religions offer different solutions to life's uncertain riddles that their RE work is confined to telling stories, 'doing' festivals or discussing vaguely ethical stories from the newspapers.

Team leaders need to find ways of building the confidence of colleagues so that more imaginative teaching and learning strategies can be developed. Such confidence grows where people can find a little time and space to share their concerns and to have them addressed. Would it help to devote a training day/CPD opportunity to RE?

Strategies to build up successful RE teams

The subject co-ordinator needs to develop **strategies** such as the following to build up the team's understanding of RE, and their confidence to deliver the subject well:

- **ways of addressing** people's reasonable concerns about aims in RE

- a clearly structured **policy statement**, devised by all those involved, and widely understood

- **schemes of work** that are easy to use, practical and comprehensive

- **team planning** that involves everybody from the start, though the subject leader will provide most of the ideas

- well-thought-out and **varied resources**, stored in usable ways

- **support** for teachers where they lack confidence (conversation, teacher observation, books to refer to, access to training and other kinds of support)

- **clarity about the outcomes** of RE work by pupils in different age groups: examples of a range of pupils' achievements and clear reference to the assessment structures of your syllabus, or to the national eight-level scale of achievement

- **agreement about the time** that is spent on RE in the classroom

- **monitoring of pupils' work** in RE (to avoid 'ten in the bed' syndrome, where one subject 'falls out' and it's always RE!).

TWOS in RE

A PCfRE project to assist Teachers With Other Specialisms (TWOs) in their RE work was undertaken from 1997 to 2000 as part of the RE and School Effectiveness project at Brunel University's BFSS National RE Centre. Among the findings of the project there was much of practical significance for any subject leader in RE, including the following ideas:

- RE is more often taught by TWOs than almost any other subject, e.g. ICT and Citizenship.

- While this is not an ideal situation, many TWOs bring their gifts as teachers to the subject, including expertise in particular parts of the RE field: e.g. historians may be good at teaching interpretation, drama teachers at engaging pupils with issues, and science teachers in tackling empirical approaches to religion.

- The first need for TWOs is to find and assimilate a professional rationale for their RE work. This won't happen without training and time to think about what the subject is for.

- RE should not be taught by the unwilling or the press-ganged. This is unfair on teachers and pupils, and is unprofessional.

- RE teaching deserves to be planned on the same basis as teaching other subjects. If there is a long-term need to use staff without training, failing the new appointment of a specialist teacher, the minimum satisfactory approach involves continuity of deployment, and appropriate professional development for those involved.

Questions for RE team leaders

- In what ways have you been successful in building your RE team? What factors have enabled this success?

- What are the most difficult aspects of building a team for RE teaching in your school? Whom can you talk to about addressing these problems?

- What do you see as the next steps forward in building more successful RE across the team? How can these be monitored?

Using TWOs can be successful, but can also contribute to low standards. Careful and supportive monitoring and intervention to change and improve the quality of teaching is the key to success.

What do you like about teaching RE?

Listening to the class argue about things that matter, instead of who's got better eye shadow.

Source: One respondent to the TWOs questionnaire.

Most non-specialists feel more confident in their knowledge of religious phenomena than theology, philosophy and ethics, which are seen as complex, controversial and to be avoided, and this limits their ability to engage pupils in some of the most interesting aspects of the subject.

Source: Ofsted, 2005.

Teachers with other specialisms are commonly used in RE in both primary and secondary school.

Such teachers can do their RE work very well, but they deserve three kinds of support as a minimum: the leadership of a specialist, the time for training and meeting and planning with the subject leader, and continuity of deployment from year to year.

Given even these basic supports, TWOs can make a good contribution.

Without them, poor teaching is all too likely.

Source: The PCfRE 'TWOs' project.

The status of RE: a checklist of questions

Building the status of RE is a continuous issue. In a secularising society, where religion is often ridiculed, RE can be marginalised. But the subject deserves better.

This page aims to help you think about how to build the status of RE in your school through a checklist of questions. Until the whole lot can be ticked, there is still a job to do.

While the list is aspirational, each of these things can be changed and improved by careful good practice.

Two uses for this list:

- **Development planning**. Use the list to analyse and set targets for your school's RE work to develop.

- **'Levelling the playing field'**. Send a copy to your headteacher, curriculum manager or governors with your comments.

✓

Are all legal requirements for the subject met?

Is there a proper job description for the subject leader, with appropriate remuneration (as for other subjects)?

Is RE provision recognised as good quality internally (e.g. by governors) and externally (e.g. by inspectors)? If not, are there any realistic plans to change and improve?

Does the RE subject leader get a fair chance to contribute to whole-school curriculum and assessment decisions and policies? Are the particular contributions of the subject recognised and well developed?

Are pupils' questions about 'why we do RE' answered to their satisfaction?

What do pupils say about their RE? Is it challenging, interesting, provocative, something they are proud of? If you don't know, run a questionnaire activity to find out.

Is the range of teaching and learning in RE broad and deep, enabling achievement for all?

Is curriculum time adequate? Is it broadly similar to other subjects, e.g. History, Geography, Music or Art?

Are financial resources adequate – broadly similar to Geography, Art or Music?

Do pupils have entitlement to go on an RE educational visit?

Can parents see that RE is a valuable part of their children's education?

Does reporting and achievement in RE match structures for the foundation subjects?

Is the work of the teaching team monitored as it is in other areas of the curriculum, e.g. literacy?

Is there support, professional development and practical day-to-day help for teachers with other specialisms who work in RE?

Does the subject leader have time to manage the teaching team?

Is the deployment of staff to RE classes effective and comparable to other subjects?

Is there a forum for the celebration of excellence in pupils' RE work?

Is the RE subject leader aware of any hostility to RE based on misunderstanding among staff, parents or pupils? Is it addressed?

In conclusion, is the 'playing field' of curriculum decision-making level?

Every Child Matters (ECM)

Every Child Matters: Change for Children (2004)

The death in 2000 of **Victoria Climbié** resulted in a massive rethink of child protection issues and brought about a more integrated approach to the wellbeing of children from birth to age 19. The aim is that every child, irrespective of their background, is entitled to the support he or she needs – to be healthy, stay safe, enjoy and achieve, make a positive contribution and achieve economic wellbeing (see page 12 for the impact RE can have on these outcomes).

Local authorities have integrated their children and young people's services (including education and social services). Part of the process also involves giving children and young people a say in the issues that affect them as individuals and collectively.

In 2005 the first **Children's Commissioner for England** was appointed (Wales has had one since 2001) to give them a say in government and public life. Many Agreed Syllabus Conferences have included reference to the implications of ECM for RE as part of their review. Teachers should draw on this for their RE planning and development as appropriate. The Ofsted (and denominational) inspection process encourages schools to take into account the views of children and their families about the education and care they receive.

The thinking behind ECM is not new to many working in education: high expectations, innovative thinking and a broad and holistic view of supporting children and young people are common features of successful schools. Teachers recognise the importance of good relationships with others supporting children such as parents/carers, social workers, educational psychologists, nurses and GPs.

From April 2006 a **Common Assessment Framework** (CAF 2006) has been developed which sets out the basic competences needed when working with children, young people and their families. Over time it is expected that everyone working in this area will demonstrate a basic competence in the six areas of the Framework and in future this will form part of qualification and training programmes.

What follows are some basic questions RE subject leaders can ask as part of the self-evaluation process in order to highlight how RE contributes to the all-round development of children and young people as laid out in Every Child Matters.

ECM: some key questions

- Where can/does/should RE make a positive contribution against the outcomes of ECM in supporting academic, spiritual, moral, social and cultural development?

- How can we adapt/improve the learning and teaching strategies we use in RE to make the experiences and opportunities even better?

- How can/does/should RE contribute to the personal development of all pupils? What do we need to do to encourage active listening and engaged response from all our pupils?

- How can we give children a voice and help them to take responsibility for their learning in RE?

- How well do we take into consideration the different religious, ethnic and cultural contexts of our children?

- How effective are we at liaising with parents, faith community leaders/visitors?

- How do we implement health and safety procedures in our RE learning and teaching?

- How effective is RE at engaging with children and their families?

Useful weblinks

- **Every Child Matters:** www.everychildmatters.gov.uk

- **Children's Commissioner:** www.childrenscommissioner.org/index.htm.

OUTCOMES FRAMEWORK - the contribution of Religious Education

Every Child Matters

BE HEALTHY

Children & Young People

physically healthy	mentally and emotionally healthy	sexually healthy	healthy lifestyles	choose not to take illegal drugs

parents, carers and families promote healthy choices

STAY SAFE

Children & Young People

safe from maltreatment, neglect, violence and sexual exploitation	safe from accidental injury and death	safe from bullying and discrimination	safe from crime and anti-social behaviour in and out of school	have security, stability and be cared for

parents, carers and families provide safe homes and stability

ENJOY & ACHIEVE

Children & Young People

ready for school	attend and enjoy school	achieve stretching national educational standards at primary school	achieve personal and social development and enjoy recreation	achieve stretching national educational standards at secondary school

parents, carers and families support learning

MAKE A POSITIVE CONTRIBUTION

Children & Young People

engage in decision making and support the community and environment	engage in law abiding and positive behaviour in and out of school	develop positive relationships and choose not to bully or discriminate	develop self-confidence and successfully deal with significant life changes and challenges	develop enterprising behaviour

parents, carers and families promote positive behaviour

ACHIEVE ECONOMIC WELLBEING

Children & Young People

engage in further education, employment or training on leaving school	ready for employment	live in decent homes and sustainable communities	access to transport and material goods	live in households free from low income

parents, carers and families are supported to be economically active

---

Religious Education makes a contribution to these outcomes through its exploration of religious and ethical teachings in the following ways:

RE encourages children to be healthy through:

- exploring what it means to respect the body while reflecting on religious beliefs about creation; investigating healthy living through religious teachings about food and drink and caring for the environment; consideration of attitudes to sexual relationships that promote the wellbeing of all

- encouraging a healthy mind through activities such as stilling, reflection, understanding prayer and meditation, and reasoned debate

- encouraging a positive self-image by enabling personal reflection and exploring ideas about the self from different religious traditions

- enabling the consideration of teachings from the faiths about drug-taking and intoxicants.

RE encourages children to stay safe by:

- giving opportunities to explore prejudice and discrimination including teachings from the faiths

- offering opportunities to consider rules and principles that guide individuals within communities and support the vulnerable

- helping them to consider whom it is safe or wise to be influenced by or to follow: who should be their role models?

- reflecting on the value of security gained from family life, from religious community and ritual, from faith in the transcendent and from other sources

- encouraging them to be increasingly able to take responsibility for who and what they are.

RE encourages children to enjoy and achieve by:

- providing a rigorous, challenging, good quality curriculum that enables pupils to learn about themselves and others through exploring religion and the big questions of life

- encountering living faith (e.g. through visits and visitors) and being given opportunities to ask and develop answers to their own questions of meaning and purpose

- setting clear and challenging standards and assessment criteria which enable all children to achieve appropriately

- promoting national accreditation at 14-19

- creating an inclusive RE curriculum that inspires all pupils, including those with special educational needs.

RE encourages children to make a positive contribution by:

- enabling pupils to explore the concepts of identity, community and belonging in religions and develop positive views of their own

- encouraging pupils to evaluate the influence of religious rules and codes for living and the meaning of being 'law abiding'

- giving opportunities to consider the nature of 'being human' and the positive common bond found in shared human experience

- enabling pupils to express their own views and ideas on all the questions RE addresses

- encouraging open-mindedness in handling questions to which people have different answers; helping to develop the ability to disagree respectfully.

RE encourages children to achieve economic wellbeing by:

- experiencing a curriculum that will allow them to grow and develop into individuals prepared for working life, able to flourish in the workplace

- providing a curriculum that offers all learners (at KS4) the opportunity to achieve a nationally recognised and accredited qualification

- giving opportunities to consider, and sometimes challenge the meaning of 'economic well-being' through studying the responses of faith to money, wealth, generosity and responsibility

- exploring religious critiques of consumerism and materialism

- encouraging pupils to continue exploring religious and spiritual issues that leads to lifelong learning.

OUTCOMES
AIMS
SUPPORT
OUTCOMES

© RE Today Professional Services Team 2005

Acknowledgement: RE Today would like to thank Lancashire SACRE for ideas in this chart.

12

Excellent and enjoyable RE 5–14

Primary National Strategy

Underlying *Excellence and Enjoyment: a strategy for primary schools* is the tenet that high standards and a broad and rich curriculum go hand in hand.

Learning and teaching need to be:

- **skills focused** as well as addressing appropriate knowledge and developing understanding
- **pupil focused** – the child at the heart of the learning and teaching process
- **rich and wide-ranging** providing flexibility, freedom (schools and pupils) and fun
- **placing emphasis** on learning and teaching (and on assessment for learning).

It asserts that:

- **children learn better** when they are excited and engaged
- **appropriate challenge stimulates** children to high standards (of both achievement and attainment)
- **children don't learn in 'boxes'** – cross-curricular skills and applications are important (especially literacy, numeracy and ICT)
- **independent learning** is important, and needs to be developed.

This means that all subjects should:

- **identify** specific skills and attitudes that the subject areas develop, both academic and personal
- **build** creativity (including problem-solving), variety and rigour into all subject areas
- **encourage** pupils to see the wider picture, linking their learning in one area with that in another.

What does *Excellence and Enjoyment* mean for Primary RE?

RE needs to develop ...

- **a well-planned curriculum** (based on the locally agreed syllabus) which focuses on the learning needs of all pupils (inclusive, supportive and challenging)
- **a wide range of approaches and strategies** for learning and teaching that are
  - active and engaging
  - creative and enjoyable.

In order to do this, teachers need to:

- **give consideration** to different and varied learning styles and preferences
- **encourage** learning by discovery and experience
- **develop** a well-thought-out assessment for learning strategy so that knowledge of the child informs how they are taught and the way in which they learn
- **establish/maintain** rigour in planning and delivering RE, focusing on the learning needs of the pupil.

Some key questions for the RE subject leader:

- Is the RE provided in my school both excellent and enjoyable, and how do I know?
- Where do we need to improve our curriculum planning?
- How broad a range of learning and teaching strategies do we use, and how do I know?
- What do staff and pupils find enjoyable about RE? What do they find difficult, and how can they be supported in these areas?

Useful weblinks

- *Excellence and Enjoyment: a strategy for primary schools* is available from: www.standards.dfes.gov.uk/primary/publications/literacy/63553/pns_excell_enjoy037703v2.pdf.

Secondary National Strategy

The **Secondary National Strategy for School Improvement** (formerly known as the Key Stage 3 Strategy) is part of the government's reform programme for secondary education to enable young people in Key Stages 3 and 4 to:

- **attend** and **enjoy** school
- **achieve** personal and social development
- **achieve** stretching educational standards.

The aim is to have a dynamic and diverse education system built on high expectations and a commitment to meet the needs of every child, underpinned by a new teacher professionalism.

Source: Secondary National Strategy for School Improvement, 2005-6, DfES, ref: 1651–2005 DCL–EN.

Resources supporting the Strategy

Since the introduction of the strategy in 2000/1, there has been a daunting number of resources for a range of school-wide initiatives. RE is well supported through these materials, both the generic and the subject-specific. **These materials include:**

- **ICTAC**: ICT Across the Curriculum
- **LiL**: Leading in Learning
- **AfL**: Assessment for Learning
- **LaL**: Literacy and Learning
- **Transition**
- **Pedagogy and Practice:** Teaching and Learning in Secondary Schools.

Review of secondary curriculum

The QCA's review of the secondary curriculum, which is planned to include RE, is intended to address the concerns of teachers that the current curriculum is too content-heavy and not sufficiently flexible to engage all learners.

The phased implementation of the revised curriculum is planned from **September 2008,** and will provide opportunities for teachers of RE to review their curriculum planning and delivery of the locally agreed syllabus in the light of the forthcoming guidance published by QCA.

What does the Secondary National Strategy mean for RE?

RE needs to develop ...

- a well-planned curriculum (based on the locally agreed syllabus) which focuses on the learning needs of all pupils (inclusive, supportive and challenging)
- a wide range of approaches and strategies for learning and teaching that are
  - active and engaging
  - creative and enjoyable.

In order to do this, teachers need to:

- give consideration to different and varied learning styles and preferences which encourage pupils to think for themselves
- develop a well-thought-out assessment for learning strategy so that knowledge of the pupil informs how they are taught and the way in which they learn
- establish/maintain rigour in planning and delivering RE, focusing on the learning needs of the pupil.

Some key questions for the RE subject leader:

- Is the RE provided in my school both excellent and enjoyable, and how do I know?
- Where do we need to improve our curriculum planning, and how can we effectively feed this into the school's improvement planning process?
- How broad a range of learning and teaching strategies do we use, and how do I know?
- What do staff and pupils find enjoyable about RE? What do they find difficult? How can they be best supported and encouraged to be fully involved in developing the subject and reflecting on practice?

Useful weblinks

- **The National Secondary Strategy materials** can be downloaded from: www.standards.dfes.gov.uk
- **QCA updates on the secondary review:** www.qca.org.uk

Planning RE and policy

Planning a scheme of work for RE

Planning is vital. Investing precious time in planning has many benefits for teachers and pupils:

- It frees you to become a more effective teacher

- It relieves stress and pressure, enabling quality teaching and learning to take place

- It is a shared process, drawing upon the expertise and insights of everyone involved, giving a sense of ownership and encouraging enthusiasm and teamwork.

There are three key steps in planning the teaching and learning activities pupils will undertake in the classroom:

- long-term planning (key stage overview)

- medium-term planning (units of work)

- short-term planning (lessons).

This section of the Handbook will give you a clear outline of the process needed, with key points to consider and develop.

Long-term planning: the key stage overview

Whose responsibility?	Subject leader, RE co-ordinator or Head of Department
What does it involve?	Organising the programmes of study across the phases or key stage(s) to ensure syllabus or specification requirements are met
Important to remember	Planning should ensure continuity and progression both within and between phases or key stages of pupils' learning.

Medium-term plan: planning units of work

Whose responsibility?	Subject leader, RE co-ordinator or Head of Department in consultation with class teachers
What does it involve?	Detailed planning of how each required element or study unit is to be delivered to meet the required attainment targets and learning outcomes
Important to remember	Planning provides a clear sequence of activities to promote progression, and includes a range of teaching and learning strategies to encourage pupil participation and skill development.

Short-term planning: lesson planning

Whose responsibility?	Class teacher
What does it involve?	Clear planning of what exactly will be done in the lesson to enable the intended learning outcomes to be achieved, taking account of the different needs of pupils
Important to remember	Develop a range of teaching and learning strategies to encourage pupil participation and skill development.

Three levels of curriculum planning: some points to consider

Long-term planning is necessary to:

- **meet** statutory requirements (e.g. local authority (LA) agreed syllabus, Scottish RME 5–14)
- **select** (if appropriate) which principal religions in addition to Christianity are to be taught in each year
- **decide** whether RE is to be taught by themes, religions or both
- **check** that if RE is taught in themes, all RE attainment targets will be met
- **organise** how the programmes of study will be divided up across the years
- **consider** how much time will be needed for each programme of study
- **plan** for continuity and progression within a pupil's time at the school
- **audit** existing resources against the scheme of work, determine deficiencies and make provision for resource development for RE
- **consider** staff development needs.

Medium-term planning is necessary to determine:

- **key teaching issues:** the key topics or questions you want to develop, taken from the programme of study. It is good practice to formulate teaching units around questions (as in the QCA units of work for RE in England) as this is an effective means of helping teachers and pupils keep a clear focus and make better progress
- **intended learning outcomes:** what pupils will know, understand and be able to do as a result of completing the unit
- **the range and sequence of teaching and learning activities,** bearing in mind that pupils learn best in a variety of ways and that effective learning comes from using a variety of strategies matched to the intended learning outcomes
- **assessment opportunities,** keeping in mind level descriptions or end-of-key-stage statements of attainment where appropriate, and the need to assess a variety of competencies using a range of assessment methods including self-assessment.

Short-term planning produces quality RE when:

- **you are clear about what you are aiming to achieve:** intended learning outcomes in terms of knowledge, understanding, skills and attitudes
- **you are able to use this understanding** to assess how well pupils achieve and use this to inform your future lesson planning
- **you are confident about all aspects of the lesson:** factual content, activity instructions, activities to support pupils with special needs, organisation of resources
- **you are able to utilise** current events, active learning strategies, choice and humour to engage pupils in their learning.

School policy statement

Religious Education needs a policy statement which accurately describes the actual practice in RE and which also:

- **sets out** clearly the rationale, aims and objectives
- **provides** all teachers with a framework
- **informs** parents and inspectors about the RE curriculum within the school.

Many schools will have a standard framework for curriculum policy statements. To adapt such a framework to meet the requirements of RE, the following should be included:

1   **Legal requirements and time allocation for Religious Education**
    - making it clear than RE is distinct from collective worship, which is not counted as curriculum time

2   **A statement about the place of RE in the curriculum**
    - an important opportunity to explain the valuable contribution RE makes to pupils' development and to help colleagues understand what RE is and is not!

3   **The aims of RE**
    - based on the syllabus (e.g. LA agreed syllabus) but indicating school priorities

4   **Attainment targets**
    - taken from syllabus documents but explained in a way which helps understanding

5   **Content and approach**
    - religions taught
    - approach to teaching religions: thematic, by religion or a mixture of both

6   **Scheme of work outline**
    - an overview of teaching units for each phase or key stage

7   **Methodology**
    - how RE is taught: an outline of teaching and learning strategies encouraged and used
    - reference to the development of skills and attitudes

8   **Resources**
    - books, artefacts, videos, ICT hardware and software, local resource centre address, local contacts

9   **Assessment**
    - a brief statement summarising how the school makes use of intended learning outcomes, levels or end-of-key stage statements to recognise and report on pupils' progress in RE

10 **RE and other aspects of the curriculum**
    - **spiritual, moral, social and cultural development** of pupils: a statement of the specific contribution RE makes to pupils' development in these areas
    - **inclusion:** a sentence summarising the school's commitment to valuing the opinions, beliefs and practices of all, and handling minority groups and opinions with sensitivity; a statement about provision for pupils in RE with a range of needs including those with special educational needs and those who are gifted or talented

11 **Withdrawal**
    - a statement of the rights of parents to withdraw their children from RE, expressed in a way which demonstrates the school's positive attitude to RE and the benefits it brings to pupils

12 **Further references**
    - syllabus (e.g. LA agreed syllabus, examination specifications, Trust Deed).

Learning strategies and challenging task-setting

Expectations

Standards in RE have been criticised for being low. A variety of reasons can be suggested, including: lack of specialist teachers; little support for the subject from headteachers and governors; insufficient time on the timetable; lack of continuity in the team delivering the subject; pressure on time from other areas of the curriculum; little opportunity for subject-specific CPD; low morale among staff.

Where standards and teacher expectation are low, an evaluation of the types of tasks set and positive action on any findings will help reverse the trend. The evaluation should be done against a background of the assessment model for the subject provided by the syllabus, and that of the school. These pages provide a starting point.

Teachers

Raising expectations can be a challenge for the teacher of RE. It may mean:

- **evaluating** teaching methods, resources and tasks set. Is RE challenging all pupils?

- **comparing** standards with those in another school, or with reference to the QCA's non-statutory eight-level scale as a benchmark. Does the subject match up to history, or to level 5?

- **ensuring** that the classroom culture is one of praise, encouragement and support. Can pupils take pride in RE?

- **allowing** pupils to take more control of their learning, to make mistakes and learn from them in a supportive environment. Do pupils choose their own learning paths and styles in RE?

Pupils

For the pupil, being set more challenging tasks will mean:

- **increased** sense of achievement in RE, boosting self-esteem

- **expectations** of a more independent approach to learning, perhaps following up their own 'big questions' for themselves

- **opportunities** to develop new or existing skills, in reflection or spiritual insight

- **increased** awareness of what is expected of them in RE

- **potential** for greater enjoyment of the religious enquiry, less disaffection

- **opportunity** for exam success where GCSE RS is an option.

Where schools have made the improvement of teaching RE a priority or have acquired teachers with an RE background, lessons have benefited from their subject knowledge and confidence, particularly in teaching religions other than Christianity ... Confident teachers have also learnt to improve the interaction between the two major learning objectives of RE: 'learning about religion' and 'learning from religion'.

Source: Ofsted Report, RE in Primary Schools, *2005.*

Where the agreed syllabus for Key Stage 3 has been made more relevant to the interests of young people, their achievement has improved. These syllabi have shifted the focus of programmes of study from knowledge of the outward phenomena of religions to a broader understanding of beliefs and the impact of religion on people's lives and society ... This move in syllabus content has facilitated the development of a wide range of skills and more challenging activities. Pupils' higher achievement is characterised by improved skills in critical thinking and discussion.

Source: Ofsted Report, RE in Secondary Schools, *2005.*

Inclusion: matching work to pupils' needs

Expectations

Inclusion is about equal opportunities for all pupils, whatever their age, gender, ethnicity, attainment or background. It pays particular attention to the provision made for, and the achievement of, different groups within a school. **These groups include:**

- girls and boys
- faith groups
- minority ethnic groups, travellers, asylum seekers and refugees
- pupils who need support to learn English as a foreign language
- lower achieving pupils
- gifted and talented pupils
- children 'looked after' by the local authority
- other children such as sick children, young carers, those from families under stress, pregnant schoolgirls, teenage mothers
- any pupils who are at risk of disaffection and exclusion.

Source: Evaluating Educational Inclusion, *Ofsted 2001.*

A broad and balanced curriculum

The statutory inclusion statement declares that schools have a responsibility to provide a broad and balanced curriculum which meets the specific needs of all pupils. It sets out **three principles** for developing a more inclusive curriculum:

- setting suitable learning challenges
- responding to pupils' diverse learning needs
- overcoming potential barriers to learning and assessment of all pupils.

The circles of inclusion

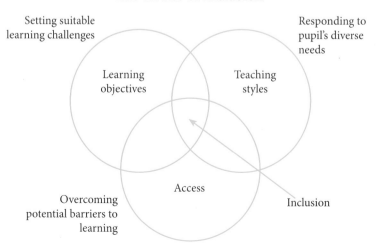

Viewing the child as a 'whole' person

Developing an all-inclusive classroom environment in RE

It can be difficult for the teacher to judge a pupils' level of need, self-esteem, 'intelligence' or preferred learning style. The information in this section will provide some tools to assess the needs of individual pupils and indicate steps needed to adjust expectations and experiment with other teaching and learning activities which may be more appropriate.

The importance of self-esteem

It is well established that self-esteem affects the way we think, our motivation and our behaviour. In the classroom, the teacher can plan an important role in increasing the self-esteem of pupils by creating an appropriate and positive learning environment. **This includes the teacher's own attitudes, behaviour and teaching style as well as the learning opportunities s/he provides.**

I enjoy the opportunity to think and talk in an environment where people are interested in what you have to say, are supportive and yet will challenge you if they don't agree with you.

Female, Hindu, aged 14

Gender and achievement in RE

In 1996 Ofsted published *The Gender Divide* which highlighted the gap in performance between girls and boys. A further report, *Boys' Achievement in Secondary Schools* (2003), found that when boys enter secondary school they are already behind girls and that in the main this gap remains throughout the secondary phase.

The provision of fair and balanced opportunities for both boys and girls is a matter of justice. But perhaps paying attention to boys' needs will help RE teachers to provide effectively for both genders.

Meeting the needs of boys (and girls): some strategies based on research into boys as learners

- use short, focused tasks with short-term achievable goals

- be explicit about expectations (set them appropriately high)

- use levels of attainment (to focus on expected standards)

- give and ask for regular feedback (e.g. end of lessons: what has been learned, what did you like/dislike)

- praise appropriately (not just for academic achievement)

- use humour

- focus on problem-solving or problem-centred activities

- provide discussion frameworks so that different views are explored and arguments developed

- use practical activities and movement (e.g. drama, role-play, games, simulations)

- use video/DVD combined with focused, challenging questions

- use ICT regularly and appropriately (see pp.86–88)

- develop imaginative approaches to assessing achievement (does not always have to be a writing task)

- use thinking skills strategies

- focus on moral dilemmas (e.g. the ethics of sport)

- use different homework approaches – not only 'finishing off' – including tabulating survey results, writing conclusions, finding out information to present next time

- use writing frames

- use RE 'detective stories' and science fiction

- manage group work effectively by planning for different combinations (e.g. mixed gender, paired work).

Special Educational Needs in RE

In mainstream schools most SEN pupils can achieve the lower levels identified on the QCA eight-level scale (levels 1 to 5/6). In special schools, the spectrum of special needs is broad with some pupils struggling to achieve the lowest 'P' levels (see www.qca.org.uk/303.html).

The Ofsted subject conference report (February 2006) states that a key weakness in Religious Education is 'teaching to the middle', meaning that those with special educational needs (and the most able) are disadvantaged. This lack of differentiation is a major factor in low standards and lack of progress in RE.

There are different approaches to matching tasks to pupils' needs, e.g. outcome (same activity different result); resource (different stimulus); support (different amount of help). **Teachers need to plan to provide a range of differentiated tasks targeted on increasing pupils' performance in RE.**

Pupils, particularly those with learning difficulties, need:

- manageable targets, broken down into short, easy steps

- to see the relevance, value and importance of their own learning

- to make progress in their learning about and learning from religion and (if possible) to recognise the progress they have made

- the RE curriculum to be accessible irrespective of particular learning difficulties

- to be given the opportunity to experience the range of learning styles on offer

- to be praised and encouraged appropriately.

Strategies to increase learning potential

In the table below, some general strategies are given for increasing the learning potential of RE for lower achieving pupils, along with an example of each.

Strategy for SEN pupils	Examples from RE classrooms
Multi-sensory approaches: (see, touch, taste, smell, hear, feel).	A small group of SEN pupils in a class of 6–7 year olds arranged a 'feel, smell, taste' activity for the whole class with a classroom assistant, using some of the special foods of Divali and Easter. They recorded responses from the class on a tick sheet for a discussion about 'celebrating with food'.
Provide raw material rather than asking pupils to find or generate it themselves; reduce research to make time for thinking, analysis, reflection.	While most of a class of 8–9 year olds researched 'Christmas around the world' from a book box and other resources, three lower-achieving pupils were asked to compare six African Christmas cards with the story of Jesus from St Matthew's Gospel, and find differences between them to report to the whole class. A classroom assistant read with them.
Time: Working slowly is a good differentiation strategy for many pupils.	The teacher set a class of 9–10 year olds a choice of tasks about four parables, asking most children to do three of the tasks set. She asked five pupils on the SEN register to choose just one task, and she read just one parable to them. Given more time, their work was more careful and was completed.
Group work (mixed or similar needs, for challenge). Through paired and small group work, pupils can progress much more effectively than alone.	In one lesson on welcoming a new baby, the teacher paired higher achieving readers with lower achieving pupils, asking them to read and report on Hindu and Christian customs at birth. In the next lesson pupils planned a baby-welcoming ceremony for the twenty-first century. She worked closely with one group of five lower-achieving pupils, leaving other groups to exercise initiative.
Support staff working with groups or individuals through carefully planned RE programmes, targeted to need (e.g. for symbolic understanding, or for considering reasons for holding a belief).	The teacher identified a group within a class of 11-year-olds who were less able than others to construct religious arguments. She used a lesson with a classroom assistant to get this group to complete writing frames about why some people believe there is no God. In the next lesson, all pupils were asked to complete writing frames about a different religious argument: What happens when we die?
Differentiated resources such as textbooks, worksheets, tasks, assessments.	One teacher always sets three tasks on school-produced worksheets, which offer simpler or more complex starting points. Another uses two versions of the same textbook, one with a lower reading access level. A third teacher devises 'tiered' assessment tasks which cover four different levels, enabling all to show what they can do.
Skip over the research or information-gathering, and set the tasks focused on other skills such as application or reflection first.	In a class of 8–9-year-olds, lower achieving pupils were given a 'head start' sheet of information about Muslim and Jewish worship, and asked to respond to 'why do they do that?' questions in discussion and in writing. Most of the class began by researching worship from textbook sources.
Reduce the 'waste' of time on purposeless writing activity. Ask: 'how could they learn this without, or without much, writing?'	In a topic on expressing spirituality through art, SEN pupils from three parallel classes of 12-year-olds skipped two lessons of written work to begin designing and making stained glass designs based on the 'I am ...' sayings of Jesus. They received a sheet of copied notes to make sure they could access the curriculum without writing, but concentrated their activity on spiritual expression in art.

Challenging the most able pupils

RE can provide the most able with opportunities to:

- develop and apply knowledge, understanding skills and processes (such as critical thinking, interpretation, insight, reflection, synthesis)

- demonstrate high levels of understanding, insight, discernment and mature reflective thinking

- engage with story, symbol, metaphor, allegory and its approach to meaning-making

- explore a range of approaches to philosophy

- develop thinking skills such as argument, reasoning and logical analysis.

Source: Meeting the Needs of Gifted, Talented and Most Able Pupils in RE, QCA 2000.

Meeting the needs of the most able in RE: some strategies

- use a variety of questioning strategies to engage pupils' thinking at a deeper level

- set tasks which focus on skills such as critical thinking, interpretation, reasoning, analysis and application

- set tasks from age groups beyond the age of the pupil

- set extension tasks which deepen understanding and reflection

- provide complex stimuli by using authentic materials from inside the faiths (prayers, sacred texts, arguments, artefacts)

- enable and encourage pupils to develop and use correct terminology and language in discussing religious, spiritual, ethical and philosophical ideas

- use carefully planned assessment strategies which help pupils identify their own achievements and learning needs

- use target-setting strategies to challenge and encourage ambitious work

- encourage pupils to make connections between their work in RE and other curriculum areas, their own interests and life issues

- provide reading resources (including identified websites) which will challenge pupils' thinking on a particular religious topic/unit.

Planning to differentiate in RE

In planning for differentiation within a study unit or piece of work we need to:

- **recognise** the variety of individual needs within a class

- **be aware** of the range of strategies available to support learning

- **select** carefully from these in order the meet the learning needs of individuals

- **evaluate** the effectiveness of strategies used in order to maximise the achievements of individuals.

Strategies

There are many strategies for learning and teaching. Consider:

- **auditing and listing** the existing strategies used in the subject

- **drawing on** strategies used in other curriculum areas

- **exploring** the possibilities by trial and error

- **experimenting** with and evaluating new methods

- **building** the strategies which work well with your pupils into schemes of work.

Learning objectives and outcomes

Being clear about learning outcomes and learning objectives, and the relationship between the two, is the key to any strategy's success.

- The **learning objective** is what the pupils are intended to learn.

- The **learning outcomes** define how pupils can assess achievement, and are the criteria for success.

While pupil outcomes will vary, it is the teacher's response to these outcomes that allows differentiation to take place.

Differentiation

Differentiation takes account of pupil differences through the process of matching work, teaching styles and learning experiences to pupils' needs. This chart provides some suggestions to support developing and engaging RE curriculum through differentiation.

Some methods of differentiation to use in RE

Method	Example from RE
Task: Whilst working on the same theme or topic, pupils tackle different tasks set by the teacher to match their individual abilities, needs and preferred learning styles.	Pupils working on the theme of worship might be variously: • interviewing believers • writing descriptions of mosques • designing and making prayer mats • commenting on the words of Islamic prayers.
Interest: Pupils are set a choice of tasks which offer different ways of achieving the same outcome. This enables them to develop an area of interest or use a particular skill such as artistic ability or ICT. Choice is the key.	In studying the ways religious beliefs are expressed in art, music and writing, pupils could choose one example, and write or record a review, or design a book or CD cover, to show their understanding of the religious meaning of the song, poem or painting. This is then presented to the rest of the group.
Resource: Independent learning and pupil responsibility can be enhanced by providing resources suitable for varied levels of ability and interest, and guiding pupils to work from appropriate books and other media.	Pupils are set a task requiring research – a wide range of different books, ICT and video resources is made available. Assessment criteria make it clear that an individual response showing thoughtful use of the resources will score highly.
Support: Differentiation by the level and type of support given by the teacher, peers and other staff. This may include: • breaking down the task into manageable steps (e.g. use of a self-study guide) • offering extension • monitoring to ensure pupils remain on task.	In an extended task on the Adam and Eve story, pupils experience a range of learning activities exploring art and animated versions of the story. They are set the task of producing an illustration of the meaning of the story for today, writing an explanation of their picture and completing an extension activity evaluating the story's lasting 'truth' for today. Levels statements outlining expected outcomes are shared with pupils from the start.
Ability: Grouping pupils in mixed- or selected-ability groups within a class may enable fullest participation and progress for all students. When such groupings are not desirable, the teacher can be prepared with reinforcement or extension tasks with varying difficulty levels.	Pupils sort opinion statements to identify those they strongly agree or disagree with. Pupils sharing a similar point of view are grouped to work out reasons to support the viewpoint – the teacher can ensure either mixed-ability groups or higher/lower ability groups to support or extend pupils.
Outcome: This will always be differentiated when tasks are sufficiently challenging or open-ended – especially if they are supported by writing frames, sentence-starters for discussion, extension questions, and so on.	Pupils asked to interpret and apply Gandhi's teaching on non-violence (*ahimsa*), and given support through writing frames and structured research activities, will elicit responses which range from a report on Gandhi's words and actions to an in-depth reflection and analysis of what the world would be like today if everyone put Gandhi's principles into practice.

Personalised learning

Personalised learning is:

- **about tailoring education** to individual need, interest and aptitude to ensure that every pupil achieves and reaches their potential

- **a philosophy** embedded into current initiatives (primary and secondary strategies) to ensure that Every Child Matters

- **not the same as** individualised learning; it involves quality whole class and group activities balanced with individual learning

- **linked**, but not identical to, differentiation

- **about adding value** to the learning journey.

Personalised learning:

- **has a strong focus** on raising standards and setting high expectations for all – this involves teaching, curriculum and school organisation being designed to be accessible to as many pupils as much of the time as possible

- **involves** giving opportunities and experiences for learning through the use of faith visitors and visits as well as through drawing on pupils' own experiences outside of the classroom

- **stresses** learning as an active social process – it should be explicit about learning skills, processes and strategies (e.g. information processing or reasoning); effective group work and probing teacher questioning is also important

- **places** a strong emphasis on accelerating the progress made by individuals and ensuring the best progress for all.

Useful web link

- **Standards site:**
  www.standards.dfes.gov.uk/personalisedlearning

Assessment for learning is:

- the process through which personalised learning (and differentiation) is achieved

- integral to the learning and teaching process.

In RE, standards are linked in most cases to the requirements of the locally agreed syllabus (some of which use an eight-level scale to exemplify this). These levels (or those of the non-statutory National Framework for RE, QCA 2004) provide a useful tool for assessment for learning.

Effective teaching and learning means:

- using a wide variety of strategies which meet a range of learning styles and needs. This helps all pupils to access their curriculum entitlement and reach their potential in the subject area.

Entitlement and choice:

- All pupils have an entitlement to a quality RE experience throughout their time at school

- For those aged 14+ having their learning in RE accredited supports such entitlement

- Appropriate opportunities for choice (of content and activity, with legal framework) should be planned into the RE curriculum.

Some key questions for RE

- How can we know our pupils better (personal, academic, strengths, areas for development) and use that knowledge to inform their learning and the progress they make?

- What choice and flexibility can we provide for individuals and groups (curriculum content, approaches)?

- How can we match our curriculum and teaching to meet the learning needs of our pupils better?

Assessment, achievement and evaluation

Help needed!

Throughout the UK, the assessment of educational outcomes has been a growth industry in recent years, whether it is testing seven-year-olds, or pressing for 'higher still' achievements and standards. Often, the rush to the assessment try-line sidesteps learning about religion. Questions posed have included:

- Is RE too spiritual to be assessed?
- Is RE last on the list for any innovation?
- Can RE teachers use levelled scales in ways that are fair, valid and accurate, without becoming 'assessment automatons'?

Some syllabuses give helpful guidance. GCSEs and Standard Grade courses enable ever-increasing numbers to get accreditation for their learning, and there is some published guidance from government agencies, but many schools and teachers continue to struggle with assessment in RE, and need further support. This is especially true for 5–14 year old pupils.

In this section, we offer some practical classroom ideas for assessing achievements in RE.

A broad definition of achievement in RE

Achievements in RE cannot be easily measured in tick boxes or tally charts. Some teachers continue to say that RE can't be assessed. If by this they mean to draw attention to RE's contribution to spiritual and moral development and the difficulty of finding instruments of assessment, or more particularly tests, that will assess empathy, moral development or spiritual insight, then a solid point is being made. **But RE teachers can work effectively with the broadest possible definition of achievement.**

Pupils have achieved something in RE if:

- their thinking, creativity and skills are engaged
- their vision of truth, beauty and love has been stimulated
- pupils have taken part in conversation about beliefs and values that is secure, calm, and thoughtful
- they achieve a wider, deeper knowledge of religions and believers.

All this is achievement, and it is good to observe, monitor, celebrate, assess and record it. RE Today takes the view that RE needs assessment in the same ways that English or Geography need assessment: **teachers can help pupils to know what they have achieved, and what they can achieve, so that their progress is swift and clear and their potential in RE is fulfilled.**

many teachers are uncertain about the assessment of RE, and need to be clearer in planning topic and lesson objectives and more familiar with assessment criteria and the use of assessment for measuring and raising pupils' achievements.

Source: Religious Education in Primary Schools
(Ofsted, February 2005) HMI 2346.

Good assessment in RE is usually associated with an agreed syllabus that includes clear assessment objectives, usually in the form of level descriptions ... "pupil friendly" versions of level descriptions, when given to pupils, help them understand what they have to do to improve their performance in RE.

Source: Religious Education in Secondary Schools
(Ofsted, February 2005) HMI 2334.

The purposes of assessment in RE

Assessing RE is all about helping pupils. Thankfully there are no league tables for RE, no comparison of results between schools until the 16-year-olds take exams. The purposes of assessing **pupils'** work in RE are clearly focused on diagnosis and prescribing remedies. We assess the subject if it will help pupils to learn more and better.

Conversely, **teachers** are rightly suspicious of any assessment structure that is unwieldy, unmanageable or focused more on data collection than improvement. School **inspectors** are rightly interested in the use of assessment information to guide and improve teaching and learning. Any other use might be a waste of teachers' precious time. Assessment in RE is for learning, not for statistics. **Assessment for learning (AfL) is a topic with a wide literature, but what does it mean in RE?**

Good AfL practice suggests teachers should use rich, deep and complex spiritual and religious **questions to drive the learning**, lesson by lesson and in assessment tasks. Pupils – including younger ones – get used to this, and learn to handle the questions increasingly well.

Teachers give **feedback that works** as communication: sharing learning intentions more, and using **comment-only marking** to show pupils clearly what to do next to improve their RE. Tell pupils clearly what they need to do to improve, and then they can try to do it.

Through AfL, teachers can help pupils develop clarity about their own performance. U**se self-assessment** strategies focused not just on thinking and study skills, but also on handling religious and spiritual questions and ideas. Pupils get more clarity about how 'good RE' looks and feels. Keep asking them 'How did you get on?' 'What did you learn from this religion?' 'What was easy, and what was hard for you?'

Teaching has a sharp assessment focus that always concerns itself with **how pupils' learning will develop**, not with how they compare to others. Don't waste precious RE time comparing pupils with others: instead spend it on helping each pupil to improve.

Assessment for learning: what does it mean in RE?

The use of **peer assessment** enables learners to develop an increasingly accurate feel for their progress in RE, and to practise the skills of communication and co-operation in the context of RE. They learn from each other, and challenge themselves to do their best.

Quality not quantity: teachers use a small number of key tasks for 'summative' purposes, but keeping the focus on improving learning with these tasks: they *assess less, but do it better*. This motto for AfL in RE focuses on the need to teach before you assess!

Teachers recognise that **RE often has about one fifth of the teaching time allowed to English or Maths** – so they do about one-fifth of the marking and assessing, really concentrating effort on assessment that is worth it.

The research shows that careful development of AfL leads to **changing relationships** within the classroom, so that teachers become more like learning facilitators, and pupils take increasing responsibility for, and interest in their RE work and progress.

Eight levels for RE

The eight-level scale is **non-statutory** and offered as guidance only to agreed syllabus conferences, SACREs, LAs and other syllabus-makers such as dioceses. Many of the most recent agreed syllabuses are taking it up (some with adaptations), and many more will follow suit in the next five years.

Schools not under the influence of LAs, e.g. those in Scotland, or Independent schools in England and Wales, may also find that the issues raised by the potential of this scale are helpful.

According to the QCA scale, the key indicators of attainment in RE are contained in three strands for Attainment Target 1 (learning about religion) and three strands for Attainment Target 2 (learning from religion). **They are tabulated like this:**

QCA attainment targets	QCA's six strands of learning	Examples of the kinds of questions this requires, mapping RE's field of enquiry (RE Today's understanding of the strands)
AT1: Learning about religion refers to how pupils develop their knowledge, skills and understanding with reference to:	**beliefs, teachings and sources**	What do people in a religious tradition believe? What do the sacred writings and key leaders teach? How are the sources of authority such as sacred texts used? What impact do they have on believers?
	practices and ways of life	What do people inside a faith do? What festivals, fasts and feasts are important? What worship or social action is involved and what meanings are given to it? How about pilgrimage, rites of passage or community life? What is the impact of these practices?
	forms of expression	Examples of the kinds of questions this requires, mapping RE's field of enquiry (RE Today's understanding of the strands)
AT2: Learning from religion refers to how pupils, in the light of their learning about religion, express their responses and insights with regard to questions and issues about:	**identity and belonging**	Who am I? Where are we from? What is the significance of our community life? Where are we going? What influences us, and how do we shape our freedoms and our sense of self?
	meaning, purpose and truth	What are the meanings of our lives? How do we find meaning in experience? What sense of purpose or destiny do I have? How do I know what is true? What do religions say about how to find the truth?
	values and commitments	What matters most to me? What do I worship? What do I live for? Is there anything I would die for? What are my values and commitments, and where have they come from?

Some observations about the eight-level scale and its use

- The scale will be of great importance to some teachers, but others will reject its use, and some will find it incompatible with their syllabuses. Professional integrity does not rest with one of these groups, but can be found in all of them. **Many recent syllabuses are using the scale, or a version based upon it.**

- It is a good scale! The scale is skills-based, does not prescribe contents for RE, balances 'learn about' and 'learn from' equally. It doesn't require assessment that is dominated by facts or by testing, but instead **permits a range of broad approaches to gathering evidence of achievement.** There are no perfect scales, though.

- Clear criterion referencing **gives RE some ammunition in the curricular 'status war'.** It provides RE with a parallel structure to the subjects of the National Curriculum. Scales like this intend to establish expectations. By describing high standards in challenging ways, it may enable teachers and schools to aim more clearly for those standards.

  Does such a scale clarify expectations (for both teachers and pupils), and contribute to high standards? Well used, it can do. In practice, teachers quickly internalise such scales and use the levels as a piece of their professional toolkit. With any particular group, two or three of the levels are important, (e.g. among 11-year-olds, levels 3, 4 and 5 may be relevant to over 90 per cent of pupils). Experience in other subjects shows that RE professionals will easily develop a 'feel' for its use.

- Do all such scales encourage box-ticking at the expense of validity? Do they undermine motivation for those who don't get the rewards of progress up the levels? Are they valid in assessing real, rich, deep, authentic learning, or only in pushing teaching towards specific, rather impoverished objectives?

  These are idealistic and genuine questions, and can't be ignored. Many teachers can cite examples where achievement by pupils sometimes blows the scale out of the water. There are 7-year-olds whose RE fits best with a line or phrase from level 7. **So the scale may judge the child, but never forget that the child may judge the scale too.**

- The two attainment targets, learning about religion and learning from religion, are closely related and neither should be taught in isolation. **Therefore, assessment needs to take place in relation to both attainment targets.**

- In deciding on a pupil's level of attainment at the end of a key stage, **judge which description best fits the pupil's performance.** When doing so, each description should be considered alongside adjacent levels.

- There are no national statutory subject-specific assessment requirements in Religious Education, but schools must report to parents on pupils' progress in RE. **Agreed syllabuses may require schools to report progress in terms of levels of attainment.** It is important to note that not all aspects of religious education can be assessed. For example, pupils may express personal views and ideas that, although integral to teaching and learning, would not be appropriate for formal assessment.

In England and Wales, expectations are that pupils will work as follows:

- Key Stage 1: Levels 1–3, most achieving level 2 at EOKS 1, age 7
- Key Stage 2: Levels 2–5, most achieving level 4 at EOKS 2, age 11
- Key Stage 3: Levels 3–8, most achieving level 5/6 at EOKS 3, age 14

The QCA eight-level scale for RE

AT 1: Learning about religion

AT 2: Learning from religion

1 Pupils use some religious words and phrases to **recognise** and **name** features of religious life and practice. They can **recall** religious stories and recognise symbols and other verbal and visual forms of religious expression.

Pupils **talk about** their own experiences and feelings, what they find interesting or puzzling and what is of value and concern to themselves and to others.

2 Pupils **use religious words** and phrases to **identify** some features of religion and its importance for some people. They begin to **show awareness** of similarities in religions. Pupils **retell** religious stories and **suggest meanings** for religious actions and symbols. They **identify** how religion is expressed in different ways.

Pupils **ask, and respond sensitively to, questions** about their own and others' experiences and feelings. They **recognise** that some questions cause people to wonder and are difficult to answer. In relation to matters of right and wrong, they **recognise** their own values and those of others.

3 Pupils **use a developing religious vocabulary** to **describe** some key features of religions, **recognising similarities and differences**. They **make links** between beliefs and sources, including religious stories and sacred texts. They **begin to identify the impact** religion has on believers' lives. They **describe** some forms of religious expression.

Pupils **identify what influences** them, **making links** between aspects of their own and others' experiences. They **ask important questions** about religion and beliefs, making links between their own and others' responses. They **make links** between values and commitments, and their own attitudes and behaviour.

4 Pupils **use a developing religious vocabulary** to describe and **show understanding** of sources, practices, beliefs, ideas, feelings and experiences. They **make links** between them, and **describe some similarities and differences** both within and between religions. They **describe the impact** of religion on people's lives. They **suggest meanings** for a range of forms of religious expression.

Pupils raise, and **suggest answers** to, questions of identity, belonging, meaning, purpose, truth, values and commitments. They **apply their ideas** to their own and other people's lives. They **describe** what inspires and influences themselves and others.

5 Pupils **use an increasingly wide religious vocabulary** to **explain the impact** of beliefs on individuals and communities. They describe why people belong to religions. They understand that similarities and differences illustrate distinctive beliefs within and between religions and **suggest possible reasons** for this. They **explain** how religious sources are used to provide answers to ultimate questions and ethical issues, recognising diversity in forms of religious, spiritual and moral expression, within and between religions.

Pupils ask, and **suggest answers** to, questions of identity, belonging, meaning, purpose and truth, values and commitments, relating them to their own and others' lives. They **explain** what inspires and influences them, **expressing their own and others' views** on the challenges of belonging to a religion.

6 Pupils **use religious and philosophical vocabulary** to **give informed accounts** of religions and beliefs, explaining the reasons for diversity within and between them. They **explain** why the impact of religions and beliefs on individuals, communities and societies varies. They **interpret** sources and arguments, **explaining the reasons** that are used in different ways by different traditions to provide answers to ultimate questions and ethical issues. They **interpret** the significance of different forms of religious, spiritual and moral expression.

Pupils **use reasoning and examples to express insights** into the relationship between beliefs, teachings and world issues. They **express insights** into their own and others' views on questions of identity and belonging, meaning, purpose and truth. They **consider the challenges of belonging** to a religion in the contemporary world, focusing on values and commitments.

7 Pupils **use a wide religious and philosophical vocabulary** to **show a coherent understanding** of a range of religions and beliefs. They **analyse** issues, values and questions of meaning and truth. They **account for** the influence of history and culture on aspects of religious life and practice. They **explain why** the consequences of belonging to a faith are not the same for all people within the same religion or tradition. They **use some of the principal methods by which religion, spirituality and ethics are studied**, including the use of a variety of sources, evidence and forms of expression.

Pupils **articulate personal and critical responses** to questions of meaning, purpose and truth and ethical issues. They **evaluate** the significance of religious and other views for understanding questions of human relationships, belonging, identity, society, values and commitments, **using appropriate evidence and examples**.

8 Pupils **use a comprehensive religious and philosophical vocabulary** to **analyse** a range of religions and beliefs. They **contextualise** interpretations of religion with reference to historical, cultural, social and philosophical ideas. They **critically evaluate the impact** of religions and beliefs on differing communities and societies. They **analyse** differing interpretations of religious, spiritual and moral sources, using some of the principal methods by which religion, spirituality and ethics are studied. They **interpret and evaluate** varied forms of religious, spiritual and moral expression.

Pupils **coherently analyse** a wide range of viewpoints on questions of identity, belonging, meaning, purpose, truth, values and commitments. They **synthesise** a range of evidence, arguments, reflections and examples, fully **justifying their own views** and ideas and providing a detailed **evaluation** of the perspectives of others.

Skills and the eight-level scale

The chart on the right picks out the **'skill words' from the eight-level scale.** This is one way of looking at criterion-referenced assessment for RE, and perhaps a most helpful starting point. Teachers who plan to these kinds of objectives will enable progression in their classes.

If pupils can, increasingly, use the skills specified here (in conjunction with increasing their access to concepts and content) then the standards of their RE work, and the progress they make, can be monitored and assessed in a straightforward way.

The skills the scale requires are most clearly seen by staff and pupils from a ladder of skills (see diagram). Our judgement about the key skill for each level at AT1 and AT2 is expressed here, and the chart might be useful for the classroom wall. Refer to the pages on progression (pp.54–6) for more detailed examples.

Level	Learn about religion	Learn from religion
8	Analyse / contextualise	Justify views
7	Account for...	Evaluate
6	Interpret	Express insight
5	Explain	Express views
4	Show understanding	Apply ideas
3	Describe	Make links
2	Retell	Respond sensitively
1	Name	Talk about

Recording achievement

In assessing RE, teachers aim to give evidence of all that each child has learned, understood and can do, in ways that are **accurate, fair and informative**.

Good practice is also administratively lightweight, not a paper-chase for the teacher. RE policy works best where it fits in with whole school assessment, recording and reporting policies.

At present, **'Assess less, but do it better'** is a good maxim for assessing RE. **So teachers might:**

- give pupils occasional tests to check their learning
- grade pupils' work on tasks such as those given above, using criteria from the eight-level scale
- use individual record cards to record learning experiences and activities
- get pupils to select two pieces of their best RE work for keeping in a folder
- take photographs, scans or make audio or video tapes of pupils' performance (especially in group work)
- devise simple structures for self-assessment and peer-assessment of skills, projects, creative activities, group work or other learning situations.

Four examples of tasks and outcomes

The value of well-thought-out assessment tasks and criterion-referenced marking approaches is most clearly illustrated with examples of pupils' work. Here are presented four examples, which show some good practice. Many more can be found on the QCA's website to exemplify the National Curriculum (and RE) at www.ncaction.org.uk.

Example 1 The promised land, by pupil A, aged 6

Teaching and learning: This class had been learning about the Exodus and the beginnings of Judaism. The teacher told the story, emphasising the 'Promised Land' in Jewish faith: slaves from Egypt were looking forward to living in a place of freedom and 'milk and honey'.

Task: Children were asked to use their imagination to think about their own 'promised land', and then draw and write a sentence to describe it. The aim was to provide evidence of achievement with regard to learning from Exodus. 'Land' is a key concept in teaching Judaism.

Level: This piece of work is evidence that pupil A is able to work at level 2 with regard to learning from religion. She can respond sensitively to the experience, feelings and values of others – in this case of Jewish people. She can also suggest a meaning she finds in the story.

Teacher's comment: She identifies three things from the natural world (flowers, sunshine, countryside) and one from the field of human relationships (nice neighbours). She uses a clear understanding of what the 'Promised Land' meant in the Jewish Exodus story to apply the idea to her own 'vision'.

This example shows two important points: first, that while it can seem difficult to get younger – or any – pupils to show achievement in learning from religion, the key to making this possible is the well set task that asks for sensitive reflection. It is worth spending time setting good tasks.

Example 2 My Special Object: The Kara, by pupil B aged 8

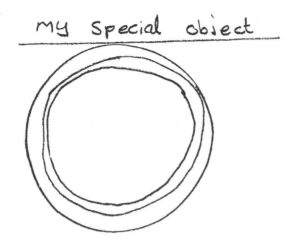

My special object

My special object is my Kara. It is silver and round and it has a lir at the sides. It is special to me because it keeps bad people out o my house so I can be safe and it helps me con sun trate when I working at home and school. I keep it on my wrist on my left hand. Th where I always keep it and I went to India I brought it from there.

Teaching and learning: This Year 3 class had been learning about symbolism and worship, using artefacts to explore what is sacred in different religions.

Task: The task was to think about home, family and wider life, and identify any objects that were so special we might call them sacred. Children were given some prompting through discussion to write a paragraph explaining ways in which their chosen symbolic object was special to them (What is it? Why is it special to you? How do you look after it?)

Level: This boy describes religious practice using the right words, and shows he is able to work at level 3 here. He identifies what's important to him, and links practice and values in the Sikh way of life.

Teachers' comment: The class produced a range of responses to the task, including non-religious ones (football shirts, dancing shoes). This variety was itself part of the learning. In this boy's work, the links between safety, concentration and religious ritual of wearing the 5ks are well made.

The teaching here has enabled a child from a minority community to express something from his own family life, and do so to the benefit of the whole class. This reflects well on the teacher's capacity to establish an open classroom atmosphere. The diversity of what we call 'sacred' becomes a resource for all pupils to learn that what is holy is different for different people.

Example 3   Learning from the Hajj, by pupil C, aged 12

Dear Gran and Grandad

I am having a lovely time here in Mecca. I've been here four days. I was going to leave tomorrow but I'm going to stay for an extra week as I'm having so much fun. There is a strong sense of peace and equality. Wherever you turn, everyone is full of goodwill and love. After prayers yesterday I spoke to the man sitting next to me. I found out that he was the richest man in the world. I was amazed as he looked very similar to everyone else in his ihram.

The Haram mosque is wonderful, it's enormous. The whole experience of going to the mosque made me feel very small and honoured to have experienced such beauty. I managed to walk round the Kaaba seven times!

It's very hot here and everyone is having to shade themselves with umbrellas. I have done a great deal of walking from place to place, I feel very drained and tired but happy because I feel I'm doing my bit to praise God. The only English thing I miss is the food, it's very different here.

I have seen the 'mountain of mercy' where Muhammad p.b.u.h. once preached. I have stoned the devil and now feel like a new, clean person. I now have a great feeling of love and forgiveness for everyone.

Lots of love from Nicola

Teaching and learning: Muhammad (pbuh) asked Muslims to show their religion in five ways: something all the time, something daily, something when you're paid, something annually and something once in a lifetime. The Hajj to Makkah is the Fifth Pillar. The teacher asked pupils to imagine themselves writing home at the end of a Hajj pilgrimage, specially taking account of the emotions of the event.

Task: This assessment activity asks pupils to describe the events of the Hajj, but also encourages them to explain the impact of the beliefs and rituals involved. It is aimed at pupils working up from level 4 to level 5.

Level: In this piece of work (she also produced a postcard of views from the Hajj) the pupil uses an increasingly wide religious vocabulary accurately. She explains through her writing why the Hajj has such an impact, and relates the challenges of belonging to Islam to her own experience. She shows she can work at level 5.

Teacher's comment: Islam is sometimes taught very factually. This activity aims to integrate the experience of the pupils with their learning about Islam, and is sound classroom work rather than a 'bolt on' extra.

Nicola's postcard is a simple task in some ways, but the way she has written shows that good teaching lies behind the work. Her contextualised use of religious vocabulary and her engagement with the emotions of the Hajj are particular qualities. In marking the piece at level 5, it is worth noting that not all aspects of a level statement can be met in any single piece of work.

Example 3   Learning from the Hajj, by pupil C, aged 12

Imagine the scene: Nothing! What does this mean? The truth is, it is completely 'unimaginable' and this is probably the reason why people find the creation story so difficult to comprehend. When we made our poster we thought that it was important to focus upon this concept. In the case of Humanists, they find it hard to believe that one higher being created everything, especially within seven days and with nothing. However, Christians can find hope and comfort in the power that God has. This is also reflected on our poster as we have shown that this higher being can create such contrasts in all living things. From the tiny ladybird to the majestic lion to the infinite sky and so on.

There is no doubt that for Christians, Humanists, and any other religious groups you could mention, this was the one of the most dramatic points in their worlds and creates the basis for their belief. This turning point in their society has enabled these people to live and this forms the foundations for the world we know today. Despite differences in the creation story [between] religions, the main focus is the fact that their higher being, be it God, Allah or a mixture of unexplainable sciences, created something out of nothing!

Teaching and learning: Pupils had studied beliefs about origins from Christianity and Humanism. Discussion had related these beliefs to their own ideas, and they were asked to concentrate on articulating and clarifying their own beliefs through a work of art and an associated written explanation.

Task: The creative dimension of this task has enabled the two pupils to show their skills visually and has provided time for reflection through their written work as well. The writing is not perfect, but should be judged positively: can they explain their perspectives in the light of the study of religion and science undertaken? The focus in the work is on the mysterious nature of the puzzling questions they have studied.

Level: Pupils D and E give evidence that they are able to work at level 5. They explain some different perspectives on an ultimate question. They ask and suggest answers to questions of identity, and use their religious vocabulary to express their own and others' viewpoints.

This is an example of paired assessment. Some teachers see this as a problem, but if both pupils agree they have contributed equally, then they can both achieve the same level. This approach uses peer work as a way of raising standards, and can be very effective.

Teacher comment: Visual learners often do their best assessment work after some creative time. This assessment task needs careful teaching, to distinguish and clarify different views about questions and origins. RE is unusual in that you can achieve up to level 5 just by asking the right kinds of questions. The quality of this piece of work lies in the depth of thought, though the drawing is lovely, too.

Foundation Stage

Overview

In England, Scotland and Northern Ireland, children are in the **Foundation Stage** from three years of age until they finish the year in which they have their fifth birthday. In Wales 'Foundation phase' describes the period from age 3 to age 7, combining the Early Years (from 3 to 5) and Key Stage 1 of the National Curriculum (5 to 7).

Children aged 4 or 5 who are on the school roll in the Reception class should be taught RE according to the appropriate syllabus (for example, the locally agreed syllabus). This does not apply to children who are withdrawn according to the wishes of their parents.

Although it is good practice to provide opportunities for 3–4 year olds to explore RE material, there is no statutory requirement to teach RE prior to children entering the Reception class.

It is important that teachers note that the requirement for RE differs from that of other subjects in the curriculum. RE becomes compulsory in the Reception class whereas National Curriculum subjects start in Year 1.

The information on this page (shown right) outlines the legal requirements in the Early Years.

Foundation Stage: Nursery (years 3–4)

- RE is non-statutory
- Practitioners may incorporate RE material into children's activities if they choose
- Early Learning Goals (Desirable Outcomes in Wales) outline what children should achieve by the end of Reception.

Foundation Stage: Reception (years 4–5)

- RE is a compulsory part of the basic curriculum for all Reception pupils
- RE should be taught according to the locally agreed syllabus for RE or diocesan guidelines
- Early Learning Goals (Desirable Outcomes in Wales) outline what pupils should achieve by the end of Reception.

Year 1 onwards

- RE is compulsory for all pupils, except those withdrawn by their parents
- RE should be taught according to the locally agreed syllabus for RE or diocesan guidelines.

The Foundation Stage

The curriculum for the Foundation Stage identifies areas of learning, known as the **Early Learning Goals** in England, Scotland and Northern Ireland, and **Desirable Outcomes** in Wales. These areas of learning outline what children are expected to achieve by the end of the stage. **These areas of learning are:**

England	Scotland	Wales	Northern Irelenad
Personal, social and emotional development	Emotional, personal and social development	Personal and social development and well-being	Personal, social and emotional development
Communication, language and literacy	Communication and language	Language, literacy and communication	Communication, language and literacy
Mathematical development		Mathematical development	Mathematical development
		Bilingualism and multicultural understanding	Early experience in science and technology
Knowledge and understanding of the world	Knowledge and understanding of the world	Knowledge and understanding of the world	Knowledge and understanding of the world
Physical development	Physical development and movement	Physical development	Physical development
Creative development.	Expressive and aesthetic development	Creative development	Creative development

The Early Learning Goals

The Early Learning Goals provide the basis for planning, but are not a curriculum themselves.

Religious Education can, and should, make an active contribution to the achievement of all these goals, and has a particularly important contribution to make to:

- personal, social and emotional development
- communication, language and literacy
- knowledge and understanding of the world
- creative development.

For children to get the most out of RE, it is important that they enjoy a wide variety of Religious Education related experiences, and that activities are carefully planned in line with the locally agreed syllabus or diocesan guidelines.

Activities which children participate in during their early years provide the building blocks for their later development. Starting with things that are familiar to children, and providing a variety of hands-on activities is essential for learning in RE at this stage.

Themes

Themes which could provide opportunities for work in RE include:

- myself
- my life
- my senses
- my special things
- people special to me
- people who help us
- friendship
- welcome
- belonging
- special places
- special times
- our community
- special books
- stories
- the natural world.

RE- related learning experiences and opportunities in the Early Years

Children should be provided with opportunities to:

- **listen to and talk about** stories (secular with a moral, religious or multicultural theme) that explore the inner world of thoughts and feelings, and which stimulate the imagination and reflection

- **directly experience** religion, e.g. engage with artefacts

- **dress up and act out** scenes from stories, celebrations or festivals

- **sing** songs to do with faith stories and festivals

- **visit** places of worship (with a focus on feelings and symbols)

- **listen and respond to** visitors from faith communities

- **get to know and use** religious words accurately, e.g. God, Bible, synagogue, church, prayer

- **use all five senses:** smell (e.g. incense); taste (e.g. special foods); see and touch (e.g. religious artefacts); hear (e.g. stories/hymns/songs/prayers/bells)

- **make and do** e.g. make festive food, role play, dress up, dance

- **have times of quiet and stillness**

- **share** their own beliefs, ideas and values

- **talk about** their feelings and experiences

- **ask** puzzling questions

- **respond creatively, imaginatively and meaningfully** to memorable events, e.g. celebrations, festivals, birth of a new baby, weddings, death of a pet

- **use** their imagination and curiosity to develop their appreciation and wonder of the world in which they live

- **begin to use** ICT to explore religious beliefs and beliefs as practised in the local and wider community.

Concepts

Concepts are the means by which people make sense of, interpret and understand life. They are the **key ideas** in any programme of study.

In RE there are two main types of concept:

- **General concepts:** these are central to the shared human experience and the personal quest for meaning and purpose. These are integral to any area of the curriculum addressing the spiritual development of pupils.

- **Religious concepts:** these fall into two categories:

  - concepts which are common to most or all major belief systems

  - concepts which are distinctive of particular belief systems.

It is **central to effective planning and teaching in RE to be able to identify the key concept** behind any particular topic or study unit, and **work out effective ways of exploring this with pupils** so that they not only grasp the key concept but can relate to it in their own lives.

The diagram below indicates some key concepts which arise in the RE fields of enquiry. Whilst we have attempted to group related concepts together, this should not be regarded as definitive, as many concepts fall into more than one category.

Shared human experience ⟶ **Religious responses**

Things we experience

Life experience
community
commitment
celebration
freedom and authority
joy and suffering
change, loss, renewal
goodness and evil
motivation
relationship
spirituality
vision

**Things which matter
most to us:**

**Values and
commitment**
love
compassion
respect
rights and
responsibilities
service
stewardship
honesty and integrity
justice
peace
forgiveness
wholeness

**Ways of expressing
understanding and interpreting
life experience**

God/deity
theism/atheism
revelation
interpretation
faith
commitment
holiness
morality
tradition
teachings of key figures
sacred texts
relationship with God

Things we strive to understand

authority
human nature
identity
meaning
origin
purpose, destiny
value

Religious practice/ lifestyle

festival
worship
prayer
ritual
vocation
discipleship
meditation
devotion
reverence

Skills

Context

Progress in Religious Education is dependent on the application and developing use of general educational skills and processes.

The following skills are central to Religious Education and are reflected in a wide range of agreed syllabuses, programmes and approaches. Teachers should plan to enable pupils to make progress in the use and application of these skills through each key stage.

RE skills	Examples of teaching and learning activities
Investigate – this includes the ability to:	• **Use a widening range** of sources to pursue answers
• **gather** information from a variety of sources	• **Highlight** important information on a handout
• **ask** relevant questions	• **Watch/listen** and make notes from video/audio/website
• **know** what may be appropriate information	• **Clarify questions** to be asked and write/email for information
	• **Prepare questions** for a visitor
	• **Explain** the meaning of words/actions/artefacts/symbols
Interpret – this includes the ability to:	• **Respond** to questions such as: What do you think it is? What is going on (in a picture)? 'What issues does the story raise?
• **draw meaning** from artefacts, symbols, stories, works of art and poetry	• **Use** figures of speech or metaphors to speak about religious ideas
• **interpret** religious language	• **Read** prayers and **explain** what they show about the person's beliefs and feelings
• **suggest** meanings of religious texts	• **Provide opportunities** for pupils to describe how atmosphere and actions make them feel
Reflect – this includes the ability to:	• **Take part** in stilling/guided visualisation activities
• **ponder** on feelings, relationships, experience ultimate questions, beliefs and practices	• **Use music** to explore feelings/thoughts
• **think and speak** carefully about religious and spiritual topics	• **Write** a prayer a Jewish/Christian/Muslim child might use
	• **Make** a 'wall of wisdom' to record pupils' insights
	• **Express feelings/insights** in a reflective poem (or prayer?)
	• **Respond** to a case study
	• **Role-play** and freeze-frame, drama/mime activities
Empathise – this includes the ability to:	• **Fortune line or feelings graph** for one character, e.g. Peter in Holy Week
• **consider** the thoughts, feelings, experiences, beliefs and values of others	• **Write** thought bubbles or captions to pictures or slides
• **see** the world through someone else's eyes	• **Tell a story** from another person's point of view
• **develop** the power of the imagination to identify feelings such as love, forgiveness, sorrow, joy	• **Hot seat**, i.e. answer questions in role of another person
	• **Read or hear or watch or talk** about a real-life case study
	• **Take part** in a guided visualisation

RE skills	Examples of teaching and learning activities
Analyse – this includes the ability to: • **draw out** essential ideas, distinguish between opinion, belief and fact • **distinguish** between key features of different faiths • **recognise** similarities and differences	• **Highlight** key words or beliefs on a handout • **Sort out** pictures of religious artefacts and symbols, matching them to the correct faith or festival • **Identify** the 'odd one out', e.g. a Hindu artefact within a set of Christian artefacts • **Match** quotations to different faiths studied • **Identify** differences and similarities between religious practices of different faiths studied using, for example, a triad activity
Synthesise – this includes the ability to: • **link** significant feature/s of religion together in a coherent pattern • **make links** between religion and human experience	• **Talk** about prayers, texts, places of worship and festivals, drawing conclusions about similar beliefs, values and practices • **Identify** similarities and differences within religions, e.g. between different Christian denominations and between different religions
Express – this includes the ability to: • **explain** concepts, rituals and practices • **identify** and **express** matters of deep concern by a variety of means, not only through words • **respond to** religious issues through a variety of media	• **Creative:** drama, role-play, dance, mime, add percussion or actions to religious story or song; make a game • **Visual:** use of collage, colour, charts, diagrams, digital video, photography, IT presentation (e.g. PowerPoint) • **Oral:** use of audio recording or presentation or debate • **Written:** poetry or reflective diary or letter or email or narrative story or newspaper report; questions for interview or visit
Apply – this includes the ability to: • apply what has been learnt from a religion to a new situation	• **Write** a story to be acted out showing the meaning of a faith story or religious teaching in a different context • **Design** own symbols • **Respond to** a case study or dilemma, for example, think about what Jesus, Guru Nanak, Buddha might do or say; what a Muslim might do
Evaluate – this includes the ability to: • **draw conclusions** by reference to different views and using reason to support own ideas • **debate** issues of religious significance with reference to experience, evidence and argument.	• **Use sorting and ranking** strategies, such as diamond ranking statements according to what pupils think or what a Muslim/Christian/Jew/Buddhist/Sikh/Hindu might think • **Contribute** personal responses to statements relating to topics in RE (e.g. 'can of worms' activity) • **Respond** to points of view on a scale of 1–10, followed by discussion, for example, a continuum or human bar chart activity.

Attitudes

Attitudes are not only explored in Religious Education, they are also experienced. Teachers cannot operate without promoting some attitudes and discouraging others. Good Religious Education encourages pupils to have positive attitudes to their learning and to the beliefs and values of others.

Which attitudes?

Many locally agreed syllabuses offer lists of the pupil attitudes that need to be fostered in RE. Comparison between them shows a substantial consensus. The non-statutory National Framework for Religious Education in England (DfES/QCA 2004) identifies the following four attitudes as essential for good learning in Religious Education:

- **self-awareness**
- **respect for all**
- **open-mindedness**
- **appreciation and wonder.**

Appreciation and wonder in RE includes pupils:

- **developing** their imagination and curiosity
- **recognising** that knowledge is bounded by mystery
- **appreciating** the sense of wonder at the world in which they live
- **developing** their capacity to respond to questions of meaning and purpose.

Self-awareness in RE includes pupils:

- **feeling confident** about their own beliefs and identity and sharing them without fear of embarrassment or ridicule
- **developing** a realistic and positive sense of their own religious, moral and spiritual ideas
- **recognising** their own uniqueness as human beings and affirming their self-worth
- **becoming** increasingly sensitive to the impact of their ideas and behaviour on other people.

Respect for all in RE includes pupils:

- **developing** skills of listening and a willingness to learn from others, even when others' views are different from their own
- **being ready** to value difference and diversity for the common good
- **appreciating** that some beliefs are not inclusive and considering the issues that this raises for individuals and society
- **being prepared** to recognise and acknowledge their own bias.

Open-mindedness in RE includes pupils:

- **being willing** to learn and gain new understanding
- **engaging in** argument or disagreeing reasonably and respectfully (without belittling or abusing others) about religious, moral and spiritual questions
- **being willing** to go beyond surface impressions
- **distinguishing between** opinions, viewpoints and beliefs in connection with issues of conviction and faith.

Developing respect for all

RE has, for many years, taught pupils about Christianity and the other principal religions represented in Britain. One part of RE's aims is to enable pupils to develop tolerant and respectful attitudes to those who hold different beliefs from their own.

Ofsted (Office for Standards in Education) evidence points to the major contribution RE makes to 'valuing diversity, promoting multicultural understanding and respect' and 'enhancing pupils' spiritual, moral, social and cultural development'.

Source: QCA website: 'Respect for all' www.qca.org.uk/301.html

- These aims appear in many school RE handbooks, but often the development of 'respect' is concentrated only in a few explicit units ... rather than being a central objective throughout the curriculum.

- Many teachers feel uneasy dealing with issues which have direct relevance or sensitivity and are subject to local prejudice.

Source: Ofsted report, Religious Education in Secondary Schools, 2005.

Almost all the primary children interviewed considered that a central aim of their learning in RE was to develop respect for and sensitivity to the beliefs of others.

Source: QCA Annual Report on Religious Education, 2005 (QCA/05/2176).

How can RE make a good contribution to 'respect for all', and impact on pupils' attitudes and values?

Some suggestions

- **Use** the statement about attitudes to help you reflect on your vision for RE. Aspire to build programmes of study in RE which enable pupils to grow in (a) self-awareness (b) respect for all (c) open-mindedness and (d) appreciation and wonder.

- **Plan tasks** that make pupils think more deeply about respect. For example, use the units of the RE Syllabus that focus on attitudes of tolerance, sensitivity and respect to explore prejudice and its consequences, and respect and its consequences.

- **Make regular and meaningful links** between what pupils are learning about in RE and the implication of these for their own values and society generally today: for example, learning about and applying the teachings of religious traditions and leaders to real-life situations in pupils' own experience.

For teachers to think about

Is my classroom a place where

- **each pupil's** identity (personal, religious, cultural) is affirmed?

- **each pupil** is praised whenever they do something praiseworthy?

- **each pupil** is encouraged to express his or her own insights?

- **each pupil** is encouraged to listen to the views of others and respect the material they are engaging with?

- **ridicule or scorn** is totally unacceptable?

- **adults** set personal examples of integrity by being truthful in all respects, even admitting ignorance or uncertainty when necessary?

What aspects can be improved?

How shall we do this?

Thinking skills

Enabling pupils in RE to **'think about thinking'** and to **'learn how to learn'** can make a significant contribution to the raising of standards, to the level of challenge provided in classroom activities, deepening each pupil's understanding of religious and spiritual questions, and adding to pupil enjoyment of the subject.

The non-statutory National Framework for RE (QCA, 2004) provides opportunities to promote thinking skills, consistent with the five expressed in the National Curriculum (2000). These are:

- **Information-processing:** pupils are enabled to locate and collect relevant information, to sort, classify, sequence, compare, contrast and to analyse part/whole relationships.

- **Reasoning:** pupils are enabled to give reasons for opinions and actions, to draw inferences and make deductions, to use precise language to explain what they think, and to make judgements and decisions informed by reasons or evidence.

- **Enquiry:** pupils are enabled to ask relevant questions, to pose and define problems, to plan what to do and how to research, to predict outcomes and anticipate responses, to test conclusions and improve ideas.

- **Creative thinking:** pupils are enabled to generate and extend ideas, to suggest hypotheses, to apply imagination, and to look for alternative innovative outcomes.

- **Evaluation:** pupils are enabled to evaluate information, to judge the value of what they read, hear and do, to develop criteria for judging the value of their own and others' work or ideas, and to have confidence in their judgements.

The **units of work** developed to exemplify the RE Framework have thinking skills strategies embedded within them.

For the teacher of RE this means:

- sharing learning objectives and outcomes with pupils

- providing appropriate structures for learning

- using a range of probing questions:

  - **process questions** (e.g. What's puzzling about this? What makes people argue about this?)

  - **speculative questions** (e.g. What do you think would happen if...? What do you think a prophet, guru, swami or deity would say about this?)

  - **connecting questions** (e.g. What do you know that is similar to this? Does anything like this happen in your life, family, culture or society?)

  - **meta-cognitive questions** (e.g. How did you come to that view? How has your own thinking changed?)

For the pupils this means:

- being clear about what is to be learned, how it fits in with what they already know and the structure of the lesson

- being actively engaged in their learning

- understanding expectations

- having a structure to work within (and adapt creatively)

- using assessment for learning to help them improve

- working independently when required to do so.

Useful weblinks

- **Exemplar units of work for RE** are available from www.qca.org.uk.

- **Thinking Skills in Primary Classrooms** (database of approaches and resources): www.standards.dfes.gov.uk/thinkingskills/.

What makes for effective use of thinking skills in RE? Six key elements

Clear objectives	Be precise about the gains in learning and the skills being practised. What do you intend that pupils will be thinking about?	Not 'know six terms about Sikh worship' but 'be able to apply three general terms about worship to Sikh practice'.
Articulation	Get pupils to express their thoughts in their words – spoken and written. 'What do you think?' is the most important RE question.	Not 'take the information given' and 'return to sender' but 'put together arguments, issues, experiences of your own'. Key role of language in learning.
Mediation	The teacher's role is between the learner and the content, extending understanding through questions, tasks, prompts or facilitating connections.	Not 'I'm telling you what I know' but 'you're in a thoughtful process: I can help you make it work better. Try this.'
Connecting learning	Seeing increasingly what it means to widen and deepen the picture of religion and life that the learner works with.	The teacher doesn't do the connecting, but opens the channels, seeking to enable holistic connection all the time.
Evaluation	Being enabled to judge, weigh up, see strengths and weaknesses. Being happy to be tentative.	Not a formulaic listing of points for and against, but a deepening recognition that big questions are contested and answers vary, but one's own answer matters greatly.
Meta-cognition	Thinking about thinking: process questions and tasks which make it possible to 'do better', to philosophise, to be a more self-aware and critically engaged learner about religion.	So teachers don't rush on to the next bit of content, but pause to examine how we did that, and what did that contribute to our skills in theology, philosophy or RS.

What matters most to Christians?

A class of **7-year-old pupils** have studied Christianity for a term. The teacher provides 20 cards with objects, people or ideas from Christianity to trios of pupils, and sets the discussion task of ranking them: What matters most to Christians; what matters less? The follow-up task asks pupils to list seven things that matter most to them. **The aim** is to get younger pupils engaged in evaluating the significance of what they have learned about Christianity, and relating it to what is significant in their own lives.

What happened to Guru Nanak when he disappeared?

A class of **11-year-old pupils** are given 12 clues from which to create some answers to this question (a 'mystery'). They work in pairs from the clues given, which include some red herrings, to hypothesise and speculate about the strange events of the start of Sikhism. After arguing their case, they compare their answers with what Sikhs say about the story. **The aim** is to engage with a key event in the origins of Sikhism through speculation.

Is God? Weighing up some arguments

A class of **14-year-old pupils** are put in groups of five to prepare their one spokesperson to support one argument for or against the reality of God. Equipped with a range of statements of the argument, they rank and order them to see which is most persuasive, and then conduct a 'mental fight' between the six groups to find a 'winning argument'. The aim is to get older pupils to articulate strengths and weaknesses of arguments they do and don't adopt for themselves, connecting their learning to a major religious question.

Creativity and RE

Creativity: What is it?

All our Futures: creativity, culture and education (National Advisory Committee, DfEE 1999) outlines **four characteristics** of creativity.

A **creative curriculum activity** will:

- involve thinking or behaving **imaginatively**

- be **purposeful** – actions directed to achieving the objective

- generate something **original**

- be of value in relation to the objective.

This means that **imagination needs to be directed to a given purpose.**

Suppose someone imagined a blue and white striped unicorn – is this creative as well as imaginative?

Not unless the imaginative idea is directed at achieving a purpose.

Imaginative activity is only **creative** if it is of **value in relation to its purpose.**

Teachers need to help pupils judge the value of what they and others do through **critical evaluation:**

- Does it do the job?

- Is it aesthetically pleasing?

- Is it a valued solution?

What is meant by **originality** when we are talking about pupils' learning? Original in relation to previous work? Or in relation to other pupils' work?

Writing a poem, choreographing a dance: work can be unique because it expresses an individual's ideas and feelings, but what about work using other approaches?

Skilled teachers help pupils **tackle questions, solve problems and have ideas that are new to them;** this makes pupils' ideas **original**, the result of **genuine creative behaviour.**

What does this mean for the classroom?

What it means for us in **RE** is that we need to:

- set **imaginative** and **purposeful tasks** that allow pupils to **express themselves** in an **original way** (tackling questions, solving problems and reflecting on their thinking/ideas)

- ensure that the resultant **work is of value** – that it **achieves what it set out to do.**

Useful web link

- **National Curriculum in Action:** www.ncaction.org.uk/creativity.

What will the creative RE lesson/classroom look like?

The room

- **colourful and stimulating** display used to celebrate and enhance learning; pictures, posters, artefacts used and displayed

- **range of different resources** used including video, DVD, CD-ROMs, music; IWBs if used properly provide a big boost to creativity

- **buzz of activity and excitement,** sometimes silence and reflection, often less than tidy but with an underlying order and purpose.

The pupils

- **engaged and active**, on task and purposeful, focusing on the task in hand and being involved

- **questioning and challenging:** Why? How? If? questions in evidence; responding in a surprising and engaged way; challenging conventions and their own and others' assumptions and thinking independently

- **making connections and seeing relationships;** recognising and linking existing knowledge and previous experience; reinterpreting and applying to new contexts; using analogy and metaphor; generalising from information and experience; searching for trends and patterns; communicating ideas in varied ways

- **thinking about what might be;** speculating and imagining; seeing possibilities, problems and challenges; asking 'What if?'; providing alternatives; looking at things from different points of view

- **exploring ideas, keeping options open;** trying fresh alternatives; responding intuitively and trusting their intuition; anticipating and overcoming difficulties (problem solving); following an idea through; keeping an open mind; adapting and modifying ideas

- **reflecting critically on ideas, actions and outcomes;** reviewing progress, asking 'Is this a good ..?' 'Is this what is needed?'; inviting feedback and incorporating as necessary; making constructive comments, ideas and explanations; making perceptive observations.

The teacher

- **acting as facilitator rather than fount of all knowledge;** willing to stand back and let pupils take the lead; opening up rather than closing down

- **also learning;** joint activity between pupils and teacher – learning role-model and modeller

- **questioning and prompting pupils;** What if? How might you? What else could you do?

- **giving appropriate praise;** establishing an atmosphere in which pupils feel safe to say things, taking risks and responding creatively

- **high expectations of both attainment and achievement;** pupils given a clear goal that is challenging yet achievable

- **holding high expectations of behaviour;** pupils know the constraints and abide by them because they have 'a stake in them'; clear and consistent classroom rules

- **conducting well-planned lessons** whilst prepared to 'deviate' if necessary

- **establishing clear learning outcomes** with tasks set to facilitate pupils at appropriate levels; lesson objectives shared with some choice of how they work and opportunity to shape the direction of their own work as appropriate

- **planning for a range of teaching styles;** during lesson, across unit, across term, across year; stimulating starting points to capture attention, stimulate interest and fire the imagination

- **encouraging pupils to review** own and others' work; develop criteria (based on 'I can ...' statements) to help them.

Creativity in RE exemplified

The creative RE classroom enables pupils to use their creative talents and capacities in RE. The close association between spirituality and imagination, religious expression and the arts, is worth building in to RE for every age group: religions revere creativity, see it as divinely inspired, or express themselves musically, architecturally, artistically and in a wonderful diversity of literary forms.

Here is one example of an RE theme which can be taught across a very wide age range. Beginning with the question **'Where is God?'** the work explores diverse possible answers from different traditions in creative ways. Pupils are challenged to express their own vision in answer to the question, in either poetry or visual arts, with depth and clarity.

RE Today and NATRE have run competitions for pupils on this theme in recent years, and display the work that results on their 'Art in Heaven' web gallery. **Looking at the web gallery inspires pupils, and models good practice in creative RE.**

A process for creative work

Introduce the question: **Where is God?** In your head, or at the end of time, in bread and wine, or in the stars, in human hearts, loving action or nowhere at all? Enable pupils to think through discussion.

How do other young people express their answer to the question? Some **examples** on the next page are useful, but many more can be seen on the Spirited Arts web gallery. Ask your pupils to choose their favourites and justify their choices.

Set the task of choosing either **poetry or visual art to answer** the 'Where is God?' question. Give pupils time, space, stimulus from religious materials and encouragement to make an excellent creative response.

Arrange for the work to be displayed and for all pupils to **explore the ideas of others** in their class. Ask: 'What would the Christians, Buddhists or Muslims say about where God is found?'

Plan **evaluation of this work by the pupils** (peer assessment?) in ways that enable them to weigh up not just the creative quality of the work, but also the theological difference that is seen in pupils' replies. Ask: 'What different beliefs about God have we seen? Why are they different?'

Four responses to the question: Where is God?

God rhymes
Taylor Richardson, aged 7

Where is God?
God is in the flowers
Using his powers

Where is God?
God is in the cloud
Watching feeling proud

Where is God?
God is in the sun
Warming everyone

Where is God?
God is in the ground
Hearing every sound

'The reason I chose this title is because God is everywhere; in shells, in animals and in your mind. You might not see God but God is everywhere and constantly looking over all the people and animals in the world, from when you wake up in the morning to when you fall asleep at night.'

Nathan, aged 10

Where is God?
Luke Steven, aged 14

God is right here, everywhere, up there.
A triangle, a tricycle, a tripod.
God is that strange young man,
blue eyes, blonde hair
Who turns water into wine.
God is a bird, a pretty white bird
Who fills people up with fire.
God can often be seen
and sometimes heard
And is beyond the boundaries of time.

Emma: 'God is all over the world, but especially in our own hearts.'

Creative projects and activities don't need to take hours, and don't have to be based on visual arts. Why not try ...

- **Creative play:** 'Can these Playmobil® people be arranged to show what we learned about Hindu or Christian worship?'

- **Creative thinking:** 'How many questions about this artefact can you make up in three minutes?' 'What good arguments can you note down in favour of the statement "the universe is not an accident?"'

- **Creative group work:** Can this group of four devise and perform mock TV adverts for the different religions we have been studying? Can the group invent a new baby-welcoming ritual for non-religious people?

- **Creative drama and dance:** Listen to the spiritual music of Hindus and Jews; move to the music in ways that express its heart. Take a story from the scriptures, and improvise a drama that sees it from three different viewpoints (e.g. the Prodigal Son: Father, Son, Brother).

Literacy and RE

Common ground

Response and communication are key to literacy, which is about developing self-expression, logical thinking, creativity and imagination as well as being fundamental to understanding others.

Religious literacy is knowing about, responding to and communicating beliefs and insights. This involves understanding, analysing and interpreting the symbols, beliefs, practices and structures of different religious worldviews ('learning about') and responding critically and empathetically to the challenge of belief and commitment in today's world ('learning from'). **Thus literacy and RE share common ground. Both, in their different ways, are about 'meaning making'.**

RE content and approaches provide ample opportunity to develop literary skills:

- **learning through talk:** discussion (in different groupings), listening (to different people), debating and presenting arguments and ideas orally are important strategies to enhance RE learning

- **learning from text:** sacred text(s) provides windows through which beliefs and practices are contextualised and analysed; written sources (story, case study, sacred, educational) provide material from which pupils gain information and insight

- **learning through writing:** different written tasks help pupils order and develop thinking in RE and develop understanding of the religions addressed

Text in RE

Different types of RE text are encountered (traditional stories, biography, parables and myths, stories that raise moral and ethical issues). In literacy, texts are divided broadly into 'fiction and poetry' and 'non-fiction'.

Whilst RE text and information books can 'fit' into these categories, it is not quite so clear where stories from sacred texts 'fit'. They could be categorised as traditional or poetry or parable, but they hold a deeper level of meaning for members of faith communities. To categorise them purely in literacy terms does them a disservice.

RE must allow for the religious significance and meaning of the text to be explored.

Taking a lead in literacy and RE

A good RE subject leader will:

- **take forward** and **interpret** the school's cross-curricular literacy policy to enhance provision and practice in RE, working closely with the school's literacy co-ordinator. In secondary schools it may be possible to identify within the department a **link person** with responsibility for literacy. This person will take responsibility for:

  - ensuring that **literacy issues form regular focus** in RE meetings (and vice versa)

  - **reviewing schemes of work** to incorporate appropriate age and ability related literacy objectives for each year group and/or unit of work

  - identifying **literacy based activities** and **tasks** that promote **effective RE learning** through opportunities **to learn through talking, reading and writing**

- **identify specific** and **on-going training needs** with regard to RE and literacy within the school/department generally and for individual teachers as appropriate

- **monitor** the **implementation** and **effect** of improvements in RE motivation and standards of work (oral, aural and written) brought about by a focus on developing literacy skills across the year groups.

Developing reading and writing or speaking and listening in RE

The following questions act as 'prompts' for teachers to consider how they can improve specific literacy skills in and through RE and at the same time improve the quality of the expression of the pupils (written and oral) in RE.

Reading and writing

Key question: How does the range and quality of reading and writing opportunities help pupils develop the skills they need to enhance their learning in RE (and how do we know)?

- What opportunities do pupils have to read and write with confidence, fluency and understanding?

- How do we encourage them to develop an interest in words and their meanings and a growing vocabulary (generally and in relation to RE)? How do we help them to understand subject-specific words better?

- Do we give them opportunity to consider different types of text?

- Do we ask them to compare and contrast different accounts of the same incident? Do they consider expression and bias?

- Do they respond in different ways, e.g. comprehension, précis, story-writing, writing for different audiences, poetry, essay, project or report writing? Do they get opportunities to draft and redraft their RE work?

- How does what they do in RE compare with the range (and level of support/challenge) offered in and through other subject areas?

Useful web links

Primary

- **Professional development materials** for speaking and listening/reading and writing are available for download: www.standards.dfes.gov.uk/primary/publications/literacy/953

Secondary

- **Literacy and Learning in Religious Education**, DfES 0668-2004 G, available for download: www.standards.dfes.gov.uk along with a range of other literacy focused material.

> I love the open discussion we have in our RE lessons. Expressing your opinions is a valuable way of communication and improving your communication.
>
> *Male, aged 14*

> I enjoy writing about God in RE. It makes me think hard.
>
> *Female. aged 10*

Speaking and listening

Key question: How does the range and quality of speaking and listening opportunities help pupils develop the skills they need to enhance their learning in RE? (and how do we know)?

- How often do pupils speak about an issue in different groupings (pairs, 3s–4s, as a class)? How confidently do they do that? How do we provide discussion frameworks to improve their confidence?

- How well do individuals present information and ideas about religious and moral issues orally? How can we improve the range of opportunities to do so and the quality of their expression of ideas?

- Do our pupils listen carefully and respectfully to others? Do they understand what is being said and use it to further discussion? Can pupils put 'both sides of an argument'? Can they give valid reasons for their opinions in an articulate way?

RE and ICT

How can using ICT raise standards in RE?

ICT offers powerful tools to help pupils to learn and achieve high standards in RE. However, getting pupils to work with computers is not in itself good practice.

When planning to use ICT in lessons, teachers should consider whether:

- **the ICT is adding value** to the lesson/activity? Would the RE learning outcomes be achieved as or more effectively without the use of ICT? E.g. **does the use of ICT:**

  - allow pupils to investigate or be creative in ways not possible otherwise?

  - give pupils access to information not otherwise readily available?

  - engage pupils in the selection and interpretation of information?

  - help pupils to think through and understand important ideas?

  - enable pupils to see patterns or behaviours more clearly?

  - add reliability or accuracy?

  - enhance the quality of presentations?

  - save time, for example spent on measuring, recording or writing?

  Is the identified form of ICT (hardware and software) the most appropriate one to use?

- **there are opportunities in the plenary** for pupils to communicate their understanding of how ICT has contributed to their learning in RE

- **schemes of work** reflect a range of uses of ICT:

  - **by pupils,** to consolidate and develop their ICT capability

  - **by teachers** to support teaching of their statutory syllabus for RE.

Building on learning in ICT

Teachers of RE need to identify opportunities to exploit pupils' capability in ICT to move learning in RE forward. The National Curriculum programmes of study for ICT group the knowledge, skills and understanding that pupils need to acquire into **four themes**, identified in the chart below.

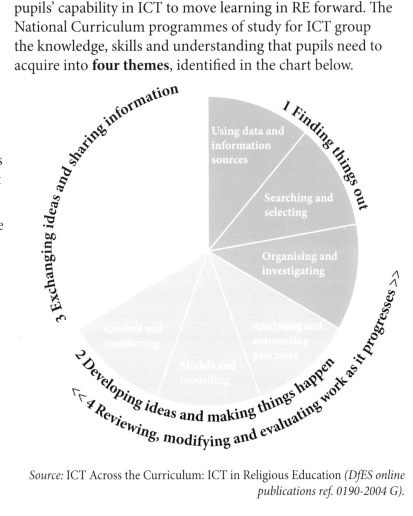

Source: ICT Across the Curriculum: ICT in Religious Education (*DfES online publications ref. 0190-2004 G*).

Of these four themes, it is the following that have most to offer RE on a regular basis:

1 Finding things out

2 Exchanging ideas and sharing information

3 Reviewing, modifying and evaluating work as it progresses.

'When we used the video cameras [to film an interview with a Hindu visitor] we were able to add more detail and effects to our presentations, so it showed we understood the lesson more. We could also compare our work with other groups, and evaluate each other's work.'

Year 9 student *on first experience of digital video filming and editing in RE.*

Communication and collaboration

Developing effective use of ICT as a tool to support learning in RE can't be done in isolation. Best practice involves teachers of RE liaising with other colleagues, and particularly the ICT subject leader.

Discussion can usefully focus on:

- **Finding out** what pupils are taught in the ICT National Curriculum. What opportunities does this open up for RE?

- **Reviewing** possible changes to timing of delivery of schemes of work. How can RE make sure pupils are building on ICT that has already been taught?

- **Identifying** areas for development in RE, e.g. evidence capture in non-textual formats. What support is needed from the ICT subject leader?

- **Working** with the ICT subject leader to identify how RE contributes to whole school policy on ICT across the curriculum. How can RE contribute to the school's capacity to achieve an externally assessed quality mark in ICT, such as Becta's ICT Mark?

- **Contributing** to whole-school discussion about the development of the school's **learning platform** (expected by 2008). What does the development of 24/7 learning have to offer RE? What will a pupil's e-portfolio for RE look like?

'During this unit there was a significant amount of collaboration with the ICT Department. This ranged from talking over ideas about possible hardware/software, to the ICT Department actually helping to teach some of the video editing techniques (in ICT lessons). This collaboration has been very beneficial to both departments, strengthening cross-curricular links for both staff and pupils.'

RE subject leader evaluating a new scheme of work

Developing e-maturity

Becta has developed a **self-review framework** which offers schools a straightforward route for improving their effective use of ICT. This **online tool** (matrix) offers **benchmarking** against established best practice and helps schools to determine an **action plan** for improvement.

The **ICT Mark** is available to schools using the self-review framework. It's an externally assessed **quality mark** against which organisations can measure whether they have reached a recognised standard of maturity in their use of technology.

Any school seeking to demonstrate its maturity in the use of ICT has to do this with regard to all aspects of the curriculum – including RE. This is good news!

Useful web links

- **Self-review framework:**
  http://schools.becta.org.uk/index.php?section=srf&catcode=ss_to_srf_suc_icm_03

- **ICT Mark:**
  http://schools.becta.org.uk/index.php?section=srf

Where next?

At the time of writing this Handbook there has been a rapid proliferation of, and interest in, **social software** – software that supports group interaction e.g. internet discussion forums, massively multiplayer online games, internet messaging, group emails, teleconferencing, weblogs, wikis, social bookmarking, mobile phone technology and more. A shift away from text to web publishing is also evident e.g. podcasting (audio – and soon video – publishing).

It is still very early days in terms of the use of social software in education. The fact that it exists is not in itself a justification for building it into mainstream educational practice – unless it contributes meaningfully to agreed (RE) educational policy. **However, 'watching this space' and 'dabbling toes in the water' where opportunities arise is certainly to be recommended for all involved in teaching RE.**

Where on the web can I find ...?

... help to embed ICT in RE

The use of ICT is embedded in the QCA's non-statutory National Framework for RE (2004), and in the schemes of work related to it. Particularly if your locally agreed syllabus is based on this Framework, the following links will be helpful:

- **QCA** (National Framework and units of work): www.qca.org.uk

- **NC Action** (exemplification): www.ncaction.org.uk

- **TeacherNet** (professional issues): www.teachernet.gov.uk

- **Teacher Training Resource Bank** (research and evidence base): www.ttrb.ac.uk

- **Better RE (REonline):** http://betterre.reonline. org.uk/using_ict/index.php

- **NATRE (National Association of Teachers of RE):** www.natre.org.uk.

... professional dialogue with colleagues?

Joining an online professional community is a good way to share advice, get feedback on ideas and talk to colleagues with experience of similar roles and situations. It is also a way of helping you stay informed (and for you to inform others) about new events, lesson ideas and resources.

Log on and see what these communities are talking about:

- **Becta:** http://schools.becta.org.uk

- **TES staffroom:** www.tes.co.uk

- **Yahoo Groups: Teachers:** http://groups.yahoo. com/group/RE-teachers

The RE Subject Associations can help too. They exist to provide professional support to members on all aspects of teaching RE. Some of their web-based information, and all of their printed publications, are available to non-members. Check out their websites:

- **RE Today Services:** www.retoday.org.uk

- **NATRE** (National Association of Teachers of RE): www.natre.org.uk.

... help to develop e-confidence

Becta supports a range of routes for schools to improve their effective and e-confident use of ICT across the curriculum, working towards e-maturity. These links will take you to the main sources of information and online tools:

- **Becta's self-review framework:** http://schools.becta.org.uk/index.php?section=srf

- **ICT Mark:** http://schools.becta.org.uk/index. php?section=srf&catcode_ss_to_srf_suc_icm_03

- **Becta:** www.becta.org.uk

- **NAACE** (professional subject association for those working in ICT): www.naace.org

- **NATRE** (National Association of Teachers of RE): www.natre.org.uk.

... resources (ICT) for RE?

Looking for good web-based resources can be frustrating and time-consuming. However, using a select number of portal sites can help provide speedy access to appropriate resources.

Check out the following:

- **REonline:** www.reonline.org.uk

- **BBC Religion and Ethics:** www.bbc.co.uk/religion/

- **CLEO:** www.cleo.net.uk

- **BBC jam:** https://jam.bbc.co.uk

- **BBC Creative Archive:** www.bbc.co.uk/schools/archive

- **Teachers' TV:** www.bbc.co.uk/schools/archive

- **Teacher Resource Exchange:** http://tre.ngfl.gov.uk

- **Schoolzone:** www.schoolzone.co.uk

- **Teacher Training Resource Bank:** www.ttrb.ac.uk

- **RE Net:** www.re-net.ac.uk

Advice on copyright can be sought from:

- **Becta:** www.becta.org.uk.

RE, Citizenship and PSHE

RE provides many opportunities for pupils to develop social and interpersonal skills and to increase their understanding of human relationships and responsibilities within society.

In these and other ways RE can make a significant contribution to Citizenship and PSHE.

Provision for RE should be clearly identifiable and distinct from other curriculum areas. It is important, however, to recognise that productive links may be made between RE, PSHE and Citizenship, both in content and approaches to learning, and that RE can make a substantial contribution to pupils' development both personally and as young citizens.

When planning the curriculum, schools need to ensure that RE is not driven by PSHE or Citizenship objectives. It must be planned in accordance with the RE syllabus, with RE learning objectives paramount.

The table below indicates some of the ways in which RE can contribute.

Some aspects of Citizenship and Personal, Social and Health Education	RE provides opportunities for pupils to:
Personal development **This concerns ...** helping pupils lead confident, healthy and responsible lives as individuals and members of society, gaining practical knowledge and skills to help them live healthily and deal with the spiritual, moral, social and cultural issues they face as they mature.	• **develop** understanding and awareness of beliefs and values and how these motivate and guide actions at personal and community level
Global citizenship **This concerns ...** enabling pupils to understand their rights and responsibilities as members of a global community; issues of social justice and equality, diversity, interdependence, peace and conflict and sustainable development.	• **gain** knowledge and understanding of beliefs, practices and lifestyles at local, national and global levels • **reflect** on the values and intentions that underpin human actions
Education for racial equality and community cohesion **This concerns ...** enabling pupils to develop attitudes of tolerance and respect for those who see the world in a different way to themselves, and promoting dialogue between pupils about issues of belief, community and religion.	• **develop** knowledge, understanding and respect for different religious beliefs, values, traditions and ethical life stances • **explore** issues of equality, justice, prejudice and discrimination, and the religious teachings and responses to these issues
Education for sustainable development and environmental awareness. **This concerns ...** enabling pupils to participate in decisions that will improve the quality of life without damaging the planet for future generations. **Key concepts** include: stewardship, needs, rights, responsibilities, values and sustainability.	• **reflect** on how human beings treat each other and their environment • **explore** beliefs and teachings of world faiths on the origin and value of life.

RE and SMSC development

RE makes a significant contribution to pupils' personal development in all aspects, but particularly to spiritual development.

RE is concerned with the ways in which people express their understanding of the significance and purpose of life, and is uniquely placed to promote the personal development of pupils' through:

- its distinctive content, exploring the teachings, beliefs and values of world faiths for insights into the nature and purpose of existence

- the learning experiences, resources, styles of teaching and the personal interaction essential to learning about and learning from religion.

The table below indicates some of the ways in which RE can contribute.

Aspects of pupils' personal development	RE provides opportunities for pupils to:
Spiritual development **This concerns...** pupils' developing knowledge and insight into beliefs, values and principles and ability to reflect on aspects of their own lives.	• **consider** life's fundamental questions and how religious teaching can relate to them • **explore** and **respond** to such questions with reference to the teaching and practices of religions, and from their own experience and viewpoint • reflect on and **express** their own beliefs, values and principles in the light of what they are studying in RE
Moral development **This concerns...** helping pupils consider, respond and make reasoned and informed choices relating to areas of right and wrong, moral conflict, concern for others, and the will to do what is right.	• **explore** the ways of life and application of codes of conduct of believers • **recognise** and **reflect** on the difference between right and wrong, good and evil • **develop** knowledge and understanding of why people behave in particular ways, why people adopt certain moral standpoints, and how moral decisions are made • **reflect** on why they choose to behave in one way or another
Social development **This concerns...** helping pupils develop their sense of identity and belonging and preparing them for adult life in a plural society.	• **work** in a range of groups • **develop understanding** of the need to live harmoniously in a plural society • **reflect** on social issues and religious responses
Cultural development **This concerns...** fostering pupils' awareness and understanding of beliefs, practices, lifestyles and values in their own multicultural society and in the wider world.	• **learn about** and **value** the richness and diversity of cultural traditions • **experience** music, sacred text, festivals and artistic expression from around the world • **challenge** racism and xenophobia • **see the worth of** themselves, their family, religion and culture.

Learning from religion

The use of the two attainment targets for RE of 'learning about religions' and 'learning from religion' is now very widespread in England and Wales. In Scotland, the dimension of personal search in RME provides for a similar focus.

Aspects of RE connected with attitudes, personal beliefs and values can seem problematic, but if the focus is upon developing the pupils' skills, it immediately becomes clear that you can achieve grade A in RE as an atheist, relativist, Christian or Hindu.

So here the view that learning from religion and personal search needs to be built up in RE leads us to suggest teachers give high priority in planning to improving the reflective, engaging and responsive aspects of the subject.

Confident teachers have also learnt to improve the interaction between the two major learning objectives of RE: 'learning about religion' and 'learning from religion'. Consequently, pupils have become more skilled at asking questions about the possible application of religious teachings and the example of religious figures to their own lives.

The broadening of the curriculum and the extension of learning from the purely factual to consideration of its application has generally made RE more relevant to pupils' lives and, where the subject is taught well, pupils perceive keenly the additional dimension it gives to their understanding of the world.

Source: Religious Education: 2004/5 annual report on curriculum and assessment, *QCA, 2005.*

Here are points to guide such developments:

Weave it all together	Learning about religion and learning from religion are interwoven in good RE, which combines the examination of living belief systems in the light of shared human experience to facilitate personal search.
Make space for human experience	Learning from religion makes space for all pupils to explore their own experiences, responses, beliefs and values – if RE is for all, then this matters intensely.
Start anywhere	Activities which promote learning from religion and personal reflection can be beginnings, middles or ends in a curriculum unit.
What do they think?	Many RE teachers could usefully provide more opportunities for pupils to give their own ideas, views and opinions: provide structure, time and space. No good RE happens unless pupils are challenged with this question: So what do you think?
No invasions of privacy	Keep on your toes, as learning from religion can, without care, slip into invasion of privacy. Pupils may share very intimate ideas and feelings in good RE lessons, but this should always be by choice. Personal search work doesn't demand you wear your heart on your sleeve.
Cut the content	Even inspectors agree that too much religious content spoils learning from religion. Follow your professional judgement, and be willing to delete the section on 'theological terminology' from term one of your course. Standards of reflection and response will only rise where time and attention are given to building the necessary skills.
Design higher quality tasks	Teachers need to spend time designing excellent classroom tasks which ask autobiographical, personal, reflective and/or argumentative questions in relation to the religious material studied, and give alternatives
Aim at the heart	RE teaching and learning needs to try to identify the core of practice and ritual in any faith: that's where the learning from religion can arise. Less work on symbolic colour and more on ultimate questions is a good recipe.
Innovate boldly	Bold teaching will be willing to experiment and innovate in personal search and learning from religion.
Learning from religion is the heart of the subject	If a religiously educated young person knows 70 facts about six religions, but thinks nothing of dismissing them all casually, then RE has failed. Where pupils get the most from RE is because they find it relevant to their own concerns and questions.

The place of learning from religion in RE

The place of learning from religion in RE is illustrated in the table below. A continuum of skills is envisaged, and the important line between processes appropriate for education and those appropriate for nurture in the context of faith is clarified. Although the diagram makes columns, there is clearly an overlap between them.

Learning about religion	Learning from religion	Spiritual and moral development in school		Nurture in faith in a religious community
Leading skills and processes:	Leading skills and processes:	Leading skills and processes:	A clear line between appropriate aims for schools and for church, mosque or synagogue.	Leading skills and processes:
• research	• reflecting on learning about religious topics	• reflection on one's own values		• commitment to the ideals of faith
• information gathering	• asking good questions	• responses to the attitudes of others		• discernment of religious truth
• factual learning	• suggesting good answers	• clarifying and articulating beliefs		• discipleship
• recalling information	• responding thoughtfully to others	• responding to ultimate questions		• faithfulness to the religion
• recording information	• understanding of concepts	• developing determination to pursue unselfish goals		• expressing convictions
• developing understanding	• application of learning	• pursuing the truth		• growing in wisdom
• defining concepts	• relating learning to one's own experience	• being tentative and at ease with diversity		• practising the virtues of faith
• analysis	• clarifying attitudes			• responding to evil
• synthesis	• articulating respectful disagreements			• taking on the challenges of faith
• weighing up arguments	• expressing responses to issues for oneself			
	• taking note of diversity in a tolerant manner			
	• accepting other views respectfully			
	• expressing personal insight in the light of religion			

Progression: moving on in RE

Example 1 Easter: a specific plan for progression in learning in RE

Introduction

Pupils are entitled to a curriculum in RE through which they can make continuing **progress towards their full potential**. This requires planned programmes of study through the years of education from 5 to 16+. This in turn requires co-ordination by those who write syllabuses and those who teach. One sure way of improving RE is to enable teachers from primary and secondary phases to meet and plan jointly. Planning for progression is also important between teachers within a school.

In terms of quality RE, topics, themes and religions may be revisited a number of times, reinforcing understanding, as long as work is **progressively more challenging for pupils.** In this section, we present several worked examples of challenging plans for progression to encourage teachers to keep on setting higher standards.

Progression in **opportunities for spiritual development** is important as well. RE can provide increasingly challenging opportunities for spiritual development. **How far does RE enable pupils to:**

- **ask and answer** questions of meaning and purpose?

- **consider** suffering and joy, hope and despair, creativity and destructiveness?

- **develop** the ability to use stillness, silence and reflection to deepen understanding and insight?

- **develop** their abilities to talk and listen sensitively and with empathy?

- **express** their own views, commitments, beliefs and opinions with clarity and in depth?

These opportunities can be provided at appropriate levels for any age group, facilitating the continuing process of spiritual development.

	Pupils might study.....	So that they might be able to......
5–7 year olds	What use Christians make of symbols like light, the cross, the chicken and the egg on Good Friday and Easter Sunday; children's versions of the stories of Easter.	• talk about celebrating Easter and celebrating festivals in their own family or faith community • draw and write simply about eggs, new life and Easter as they make Easter cards.
8–10 year olds	Some biblical stories of Jesus' trial, death and resurrection, through the art and music of Christians in today's church.	• design and make a symbolic 'resurrection' sculpture, window or painting • show their learning about Christian understandings of hopes for the future, making links to their own experience.
11–13 year olds	The place of the Eucharist and the celebration of Easter in two different Christian denominations from different countries, and the roots of these aspects of worship in the gospels; the beliefs (for example about forgiveness) which are expressed at Eucharist and Easter.	• explain some ways in which the Eucharist relates to Jesus' last supper, and the Easter festival to his resurrection • consider and explain the significance of the Easter events for Christians • relate Easter ideas to their own thinking about forgiveness, remembrance and hope.
14–16 year olds	Christian doctrines of salvation from sin, and their relationship to the death and resurrection of Jesus; the teaching of another religion about the human condition.	• develop answers to questions about what Christians believe about life after death • relate these ideas to the gospel accounts of the resurrection of Jesus • explain what is distinctive and what is common in Christian and other accounts of life after death.
18 year olds	Debates within Christianity about the historicity and theology of Easter.	• express their own personal and critical evaluation of the place of Easter within the Christian faith • philosophise about the idea of life after death.

Example 2   Learning from the Qur'an – belief and practice in Islam

	Pupils might study.....	So that they might be able to......
5–7 year olds	Posters, videos and artefacts from which they can learn how the Qur'an is treated and used: the Qur'an as a holy book.	• recognise the Qur'an is a special book for Muslims containing the word of Allah • think about the meaning of 'holy' and 'sacred' for themselves.
8–10 year olds	The story of the Prophet Muhammad (pbuh) receiving the Qu'ran. How did this change his life and that of his followers? How is the Qur'an used in Muslim communities? The Qur'an as a gift of Allah.	• know and understand Muslims believe Muhammad to be the last prophet of Allah • understand that the Qur'an guides how Muslims lead their lives • think about sources of guidance in their own lives.
11–13 year olds	Explore some sayings in the Qur'an. Discover how the Hadith may be used in relation to the Qur'an. The Qur'an as a source of authority.	• understand more fully how Muslims live their lives, and explain their views • compare the teachings found in the Qur'an and the Hadith with that of another faith or faiths, and with their own beliefs and values.
14–16 year olds	Examine the role of women and men in Islam with reference to the Qur'an. The Qur'an's role in ethics and social practice, law and culture.	• express insights and interpretations of their own in the light of their study of Qur'anic teaching • compare Islamic and 'western' ideas about ethics and society, expressing their own ideas and values.
18 year olds	Examine the differences within Islam with reference to the Qur'an and Islamic text. The Qur'an's impact as philosophers or sociologists might see it.	• identify and understand the tensions and diversity within Muslim communities, using the methods of philosophy or sociology • evaluate personally and critically the impact of the Qur'an on Islamic life.

Of all the religions studied in RE, Islam is perhaps most in danger of being treated too 'safely'. In an Islamaphobic society, even RE teachers may be tempted to stick to the facts, ignoring the wider needs of pupils to really engage with difference, disagreement and controversy.

This is a shame, because Islam is a rich and rewarding source of questions, issues and contrasts for any young person growing up in the UK at the start of the twenty-first century.

So a progressed study of Islam will increasingly challenge pupils to:

• relate their learning to their own interpretation of the wider world

• examine the challenges Muslims face, and present, in Britain today.

Developing progression

Teachers might:

• **use or adapt** the grid on pages 57, 58 and 59 to **review** the way pupils learn about a theme, a religion or a concept over several years.

• **ensure** that pupils are clear about the development of their learning; **ask** pupils what confuses them in RE, or what they don't understand about the subject to find out where to start!

• **use Example 2** to consider curriculum development for clearer progression at your school. Do the general descriptors clarify the issues of continuity and progression? What use could you make of them?

• **think through** the need to keep returning to the central core concepts of RE (e.g. God, religion, worship, belief, sacred texts, ethics, authority) in ways that enable pupils to make continuing progress.

Example 3 Progression in questioning

	Pupils might study.....	**So that they can...**
5–8 year olds	**Questions** that puzzle us: activities to enable curiosity to run wild around spiritual and religious topics. **Stories** from faith to answer puzzling questions (e.g. creation stories, stories about dying).	• make up three questions they would like to ask 'the person who knows everything' • talk about the things that puzzle them about the world • speculate ('I wonder...') about life's big mysteries • hear a story that gives a spiritual answer to a spiritual question.
9–11 year olds	**Asking big questions:** Pupils use the answers two religions give to their 'big questions' about God, life and where we come from to compare and to develop their own answers to the questions in the light of their learning. **Stories that teach beliefs:** activities that unpack the beliefs behind stories about the big and puzzling questions. **Mysteries:** activities that show that knowledge is bounded by mystery.	• talk thoughtfully about a 'big question' in a pair or group, linking their ideas to ideas from a religion they have studied • make a link between their own ideas and those of someone they disagree with • identify an experience which might lead to a belief. • recognise that a belief can be expressed through a story, and give an example of this • discuss some mysterious spiritual questions and describe their own views, and the views of someone else.
12–14 year olds	**Similar and different:** Pupils engage in activities that alert them to similarities and differences between religions in their answers to ultimate questions. **Reasons and experiences:** Learn that opinions can be supported by identifying reasons and experiences that confirm or influence their own ideas and those of others. **Arguments:** Develop their skills in argument, so that their answers to ultimate questions begin to move beyond mere opinion to philosophy or theology.	• discuss what is similar and different between reincarnation and eternal life in Hindu and Christian traditions • make lists of similarities and difference between Buddhist and Muslim answers to the question 'Why do we suffer?' • show they understand how people's experience of the presence of God may influence their beliefs • give five reasons why Muslim people choose to fast in Ramadan, and five to explain why Christmas is the most popular Christian festival • express three arguments for the idea that 'God is love', and three against • argue the case for their view about government funding for religiously based community projects, clearly and thoughtfully (social questions can lead to ultimate issues too).
14–16 year olds	**Insight:** ways of expressing their own spiritual insights in the light of what religions teach. **Evaluation:** issues and questions that require balanced understanding. **Analysis:** the skills of taking a question to pieces through philosophy, and putting it back together again. **Balanced conclusions:** the importance of recognising the strengths of different positions.	• ask insightful questions about some ultimate issues, and suggest reasoned responses to religious viewpoints • evaluate different answers to the 'mystery of origins' using reasoning and evidence • analyse some spiritual questions ('Do we have souls?' 'Does atheism make you more moral than theism?') using philosophical methods • balance the conclusions they draw by referring to the views and arguments of others.

This example of progression focuses on the difficult process of getting pupils involved in tackling religious and spiritual questions for themselves.

Ultimate questions are those that have no certain agreed answers, and are central to the visions of life found in religions. Such questions are right at the heart of AT2, learning from religion.

If the personal search of each pupil is to be facilitated through RE, then links, connections, similarities and differences in questions and answers must be studied.

This is not easy, but the table gives some approaches and examples which work.

RE for all: 14–19 and examinations in RS

Entitlements to religious education are established in law in the UK. For example, all pupils on school rolls in England and Wales must be provided with RE, including all 14–19s (see p.6). This provides RE with a precious opportunity and a responsibility.

While most of the students will take a certificated course in RE, RME or RS in the 14–16 years, many schools struggle to provide the entitlement effectively for 16–19s.

It's worth thinking about the spiritual needs and educational needs of young people 14–19: what will best meet their needs in the light of the law? So teachers in secondary schools need to consider carefully the merits and disadvantages of using public examinations for RE

Choosing a course

Quality RE can be found on both sides of this continuing argument. Those wanting to explore and develop their use of examinations might consider:

- Does the course match the expertise of teachers?

- Does the course meet the needs of all the students, bearing in mind differentiation, religious backgrounds and relevance?

- Is the assessment pattern flexible (check coursework, styles of questions in exams, and so on) so as to enable students to show what they know, understand and can do?

- Does the course enable the school to fulfil its legal obligations, for example with regard to an agreed syllabus?

- Is the course well supported by the examination awarding body, training opportunities and published resources, including broadcasts and ICT?

Advantages

- Working towards an examination gives RE/RS/RME status in the pupil's eyes.

- Qualifications such as Entry Levels, GCSE, Standard Grade, Highers and AS/A2 levels credit students' achievements and make them clear to the adult world and the world of work.

- National syllabuses and external assessment can make RE more rigorous.

- National resource providers and publishers often give of their best in the examination syllabus resources they offer.

- An RE department may strengthen its status and position in a school through examination success.

- Examination success at 16+ may encourage young people to study religion at higher levels, or even become RE teachers!

Disadvantages

- National examinations may not fit well with local syllabuses, or the local needs of your pupils.

- GCSE and Standard Grade syllabuses do not cater for the full ability range, and RE needs to offer access and opportunities to pupils of all abilities. Entry Levels and vocational units may supplement these.

- Working to an examination syllabus constrains what goes on in the RE classroom, leaving too little time for focus upon, for example, personal search, spiritual development or affective learning.

- The educational culture of over–assessment and functionalism is less likely to be challenged from RE if the subject buys into examination culture.

Qualifications at 14+

In Scotland, students may take Standard Grade Religious Studies. Scottish candidates may also get a qualification for a short course in religious and moral education involving 40 hours of tuition.

In England and Wales, the curriculum authorities permit GCSE examinations in Religious Studies as a full course, requiring about 140 hours of tuition, or a short course, requiring about 70 hours of tuition.

There is a wide choice of subjects, religions and structures for study in all these examinations from the various awarding bodies.

The English National Framework provides a clear picture of 14–16 RE's scope and field of enquiry, for the guidance of syllabus makers.

A rising trend

Numbers taking all these qualifications are rising currently, as part of a modest resurgence in Religious Education in the UK. The example in the table below shows the growth of 14+ national certification in England and Wales over recent years.

England and Wales: Full and Short Course growth in GCSE RS/RE, 1987–2006

	1987	1992	1997	2002	2006
GCSE Full Course	87 000	101 000	113 000	122 000	**160 000**
GCSE Short Course	-	-	12 000	201 000	**271 000**
Total GCSE Entry	87 000	101 000	125 000	323 000	**431 000**

Options at 14+

A very extensive range of options for studying for national qualifications at 16+ is available, and teachers should check them with the relevant awarding bodies. The list on the right gives a simple summary of some of the topics addressed.

Courses may focus on the belief and practice of one or two religions, or upon the religious responses to social and ethical questions and the fundamental questions of life.

Teachers should refer to the published specifications of three English awarding bodies, one in Wales and the Scottish Qualifications Authority. These have changed several times in the last few years, and may continue to be revised.

Qualifications at 16+

Scottish Highers and AS and A2 levels in England and Wales are available from various examining boards in Religious Studies. Again a wide variety of options is available, including a range of biblical studies, religious philosophy and ethics, the study of one from six world religions and some studies of contemporary and historical religious, social and psychological issues.

Again, numbers taking these courses have been increasing steadily in the last 10 years: around 18,500 students were working at AS level in England and Wales in 2006, double the number from 1997.

Religion and...

...environment

...wealth and poverty

...crime and punishment

...medical ethics

...the media

...sexual ethics

...family life

...human equality

...social responsibility

...science

...spirituality

...the nature of belief

...death and afterlife

...good and evil

...identity

...authority and belief

...expression in the arts

...community

...celebration

...lifestyle

...sacred texts

Provision of 16–19 RE for all

All students on the roll of schools in England and Wales have an entitlement to RE (unless they are withdrawn from the subject by their parents). For many school sixth forms, student indifference and hostility is reinforced in the staffroom, and the entitlement is not met, leading to critical comments from inspectors.

It is no easier to make this provision at high quality than to meet other entitlements, to sex education, careers guidance, PE or Citizenship, but ignoring these enriching aspects of the curriculum impoverishes schools and students.

One recent initiative, from the Christian communities, is *dare2engage* (www.dare2engage.org), providing resources, ideas and examples of successful RE for all, 16–19.

How?

The three main types of provision for Religious Education at post 16 are:

Examination courses in Religious Studies

RE modules delivered within General Studies or vocational courses

Enrichment courses: non-examination courses which are taken alongside courses leading to accreditation.

Schools may select any combination of the following types of provision:

- weekly sessions
- modules in a cycle of enrichment studies
- day conferences dedicated to the exploration of religious and spiritual questions.

Why?

Aside from the legal requirement, the educational rationale for RE for all 16–19 can make reference to:

The importance of a curriculum that is broad, rich and encompasses the spiritual and moral as well as the work-related.

The contributions of RE to multicultural and anti-racist education for community cohesion.

The examination of ethical, spiritual and religious dimensions of all other curricular subjects.

The value of study that is mind-broadening and focused on human identity and purpose rather than the world of work.

The inherent challenge and fascination of the study of religious and spiritual aspects of humanity.

What can be studied?

The range of subject matter and learning styles can be very broad at this stage of education. Open-endedness, challenge and interactivity in learning are keys to success. For example, we have run programmes on subjects such as:

Is God? What is the nature of claims to know or experience God? What shapes or meanings of a Godless universe can be described? Do transcendent experiences imply something about God, or something about humanity? What can we learn from (e.g.) Sikhs and Christians about these questions?

Why evil? What do we mean by evil, and how do we explain it? What reduces moral evils like prejudice or genocide, poverty or sexism? What insights do (e.g.) Buddhists, Christians and Jews have to offer?

God, ethics and sexuality: What kinds of authority in sexual morality do you reject? And accept? What makes for wellbeing in sex ethics, and what for destructiveness? What can be learned from the study of Islamic, Humanist and Christian approaches to sex ethics? What is body theology, and what attitudes to the body make sense of my life? Why is cosmetic surgery a popular fantasy?

Faith in the future: What is the future of religion, and the alternatives to religion? What stories of religious growth and decline do we find persuasive from sociology, psychology, politics and theology?

The politics of religion: What accounts of religion as repressive and liberating are to be found in our media and public life? How are film and media portraying and using religious and spiritual ideas for entertainment, politics, advertising or control? Does religion set people free, or tie them down?

Within Religious Education there is an inevitable tension between the two words 'religious' and 'education'. Historically it has always been the case that people were inducted into a particular faith community, not religiously educated in a range of faiths.

When the subject began to develop a truly educational rationale, it did so by distancing itself from its subject matter – religion. This led to an approach that emphasised learning about religions but was wary of any suggestion that pupils might learn from the religions they studied.

If, however, our concern is to facilitate the personal search of our pupils, we must expect that they will learn from the world faiths as well as learning about them. What we are trying to achieve in pupils has been described as critical solidarity – an ability to stand alongside the members of a faith community while still retaining objectivity.

As religious educators we tread a tightrope between engagement and objectivity. We have to see faiths as an outsider would see them and retain the ability as educators to make judgements as to what, from which faiths, will offer our pupils the greatest possibilities for personal growth.

Selection and treatment

The RE Today Professional Services team takes the view that the **key issues** relate to the selection and treatment of materials from the faith communities.

The process of selection will, of course, already have started in the syllabus (e.g. the Local Authority Agreed Syllabus), which may require certain elements of certain faiths to be addressed at particular stages. Many syllabuses, however, offer choices to schools that may leave them large measures of freedom.

Even where the content has been fairly tightly prescribed by the syllabus, there may be many different ways of treating it.

In Islam, for example, a treatment of hajj which focuses on the spiritual growth such a journey can inspire will be much more effective than one which concentrates almost entirely on mechanical details.

In deciding on the selection of material and its treatment, there are **two criteria** to be considered:

- Will this present a true picture of what is important to the members of the faith community itself?

- How much potential does this have for promoting the spiritual growth of pupils regardless of their own faith (or non-faith) stance?

A working code

The school might think about adopting a policy statement such as the one below with regard to the treatment of faith communities in RE.

With regard to the way in which it represents faith communities, the school will:

- **present** accurate information about the faith, both in its historical development and as it is practised today

- **convey** how the faith is understood from within

- **focus** on key beliefs, values and practices as identified by the faith community itself

- **indicate** the variety of ways in which individual believers may respond to the demands of their faith

- **involve,** as far as is practicable, practitioners of the faith to provide an authentic 'insider' view, while recognising that there may be a variety of 'insider' views

- **endeavour** to achieve clarity about how faiths differ from one another while also pointing to areas of common ground.

The key issue for schools is that there is evidence to suggest that RE is a primary contributor to 'respect for all' in the curriculum. This should be a further reminder to schools that RE must be subject to the same levels of scrutiny and the same high expectations as other subjects. It is clear from pupils' own reflections that those who receive poor quality RE stand to lose more than knowledge and understanding.

Source: Ofsted report, RE in Secondary Schools, *2005.*

Implications for methodology

Another section of this book deals with teaching methods and task-setting in RE but it is worth noting that the approach to world faiths identified here has unavoidable implications for methodology.

If the purpose of RE is to help pupils advance in their personal search for meaning through reflection on shared human experience and the insights of the major faiths, they are unlikely to achieve this through a heavily content-laden curriculum.

Pupils are most likely to advance in self-understanding by meeting with members of faith communities, by questioning, by reflecting, by imagining, by doing, by expressing.

The methodologies most appropriate for RE will be the ones that engage the pupil in a process of discovery. Of course facts have their part to play in any programme of Religious Education, as in any other subject, but always the question needs to be asked: 'What will the pupil do with this fact?'

Questions for the RE classroom

What can be learned about:

- **writings** that are considered sacred?
- **stories** told about God or the gods?
- **buildings** used for worship?
- **artefacts** and the meanings they convey?
- **ceremonies** and **celebrations?**
- **community life?**
- **faith** being put into practice in daily life?

What can be learned by asking:

- **what** does this mean to a believer?
- **how** might this change a believer's life?
- **what** beliefs, concepts or values does this practice point to?
- **how** does this relate to my search for significance?

Which pupil would you like to have taught?

Three pupils, having left different schools aged 16, fall into conversation at the job centre about their qualifications and schools …

Abby says:

'We did RE at school. I know loads about all the different religions. I think we studied about six, and although it was interesting to know what happens at a Buddhist funeral, I don't think it's going to help me get a job.'

Ben comments:

'It wasn't like that at our school: we did citizenship and careers along with a course about beliefs. I never really learned about particular religions very much, more just about issues like abortion and poverty. It was interesting, but I never knew why it was called religious education, really.'

Cassie says:

'I'm surprised – we didn't do many religions, just about Christians and Muslims, but it made me think a lot about my own ideals. I'm not religious myself, but I always enjoyed looking at the points of view in Christianity or Islam and reacting to them. I liked RE – it made me think about my own life more than any other subject.'

Buddhists

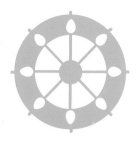

Buddhism – a brief outline

Buddhism was founded by an Indian Prince, Siddattha Gotama, who lived in the sixth century BCE. He was brought up in luxury, but when he encountered suffering he left his palace and spent his life in the search for answers to the questions posed by human life.

After following severe and ascetic practices for some years, he came to realise that a Middle Way of compassion to oneself and others leads to enlightenment. The path he taught his followers for remaining 40 years of his life showed a way to liberation from suffering.

Following his enlightenment at the age of 35, Siddattha Gotama was given the title 'Buddha' (meaning 'enlightened one') by his disciples. Another name that is given to him is Shakyamuni (meaning 'wise man of the Shakya clan').

The Buddha is greatly honoured for his teaching, but is not worshipped as God. Buddhists do not pray to Buddha. It is possible to be an atheist and follow the Buddhist path.

The Four Noble Truths

- **Life involves suffering (*dukkha*) until enlightenment.** It is not difficult to see that there is suffering and unhappiness in life, both in the world at large and within our own selves.

- **The causes of suffering are desires.** We do not like suffering and unhappiness: it is what we want to move away from. To do this, we need to understand and remove its causes.

- **The end of suffering (niroda) is possible – by replacing craving and desire with inner satisfaction.** The point at which this is achieved is called *Nirvana*, a state of peace and happiness. This is a goal which all can move towards.

- **Following the Eightfold Path leads to Nirvana, and the cessation of suffering.** This is the path of growth and development that enables us to cultivate the positive in all aspects of our lives. The Buddha warned in the Dhammapada, a famous Buddhist teaching, that it is the obligation of the individual to make the effort to follow this path.

The Buddhist way

The Buddhist way involves:

- the **Four Noble Truths** (understanding the causes and the cure of suffering)

- the **Noble Eightfold Path** (following a way of life which points the way to the end of suffering)

- **ethics** (precepts to follow)

- **meditation**

The Three Treasures (Refuges)

Buddhists take refuge in three treasures:

- **the Buddha**

- the **Dhamma** (the teaching)

- the **Sangha**

The Noble Eightfold Path

• Right understanding	steps to wisdom
• Right thought	
• Right speech	ethical steps
• Right action	
• Right livelihood	
• Right effort	mental steps
• Right mindfulness	
• Right concentration	

While Buddhist monks are often highly visible, most Buddhists follow the path as lay people. The community shares the task of alleviating suffering, supports its monks and nuns, recognises and supports its leaders and celebrates such festivals as Wesak, remembering the birth, enlightenment and passing away of the Buddha.

Many Buddhists do not attend temples, but worship in shrines in their homes or gardens. This factor means that it is difficult to estimate accurately the true number of Buddhists in the world today.

Enlightenment

The unifying belief of all Buddhists is the enlightenment experience of the Buddha. Enlightenment is not a place, but a state of being, based on wisdom and compassion. It is to do with learning Truth for yourself.

Unless someone gains enlightenment, Buddhists believe that she or he will continue to be reborn. Breaking out of this cycle is known as Nirvana.

Schools within Buddhism

There are two main schools within Buddhism:

- **Theravada Buddhism,** meaning teachings of the elders

- **Mahayana Buddhism,** meaning great vehicle.

Often, Theravada Buddhists will live as monks and nuns, free from the distractions of family commitments. Mahayana Buddhists believe that there are many ways of reaching enlightenment.

Buddhism today

From its beginnings in India, many schools and traditions developed within Buddhism. The Buddhist path is very influential in India, China, Japan, Thailand, Tibet, Burma, Sri Lanka and many other countries. Towards the end of the nineteenth century, Buddhism began to be practised in Britain, and Buddhist traditions from all of the above countries have found expression here.

Worldwide: approximately 360,000,000.

In Britain: approximately 130,000.

The Five Precepts (Pansil)

These are not commandments, but guidance to be followed by all Buddhists. They are not simply negatives, but encourage a positive moving forwards.

Buddhists should refrain from:
- harming or killing living beings

- stealing

- intoxicants (like alcohol, drugs or tobacco)

- sexual misconduct

- wrong speech.

Monks and nuns have a further five precepts.

They should refrain from:
- eating after midday

- dancing, singing and watching unsuitable entertainments

- using scents or perfumes

- sleeping on luxurious beds

- handling gold or silver.

Buddhism in the classroom

It is appropriate for pupils of any school age to study Buddhism. Many syllabuses require this, and others make it optional.

Teachers will be able to find many good classroom resources (e.g. books, posters, artefacts, DVDs, videos and websites) for the engaging, challenging and active teaching of Buddhism.

A balanced programme of study should include material that aims to develop understanding of:

- the Buddha

- teaching, beliefs and values

- festivals, rituals and practices

- Buddhists in Britain today.

The ideas on the next page suggest some activities for teachers with different age groups to plan active RE work with a focus on Buddhism. They are intended to be used flexibly.

Work with 6–8 year olds

- **Retell** stories.
  Ask: What happened to the young Prince Siddattha to make him leave his palace?

- **Explore** two images of the Buddha.
  Ask: Why do they look the way they do? What are they used for? Who values them?

- **Think** about not causing harm.
  Talk about killing and hurting.
  Ask: Why does this happen? Could it be stopped?

- **Make** a 'wheel', or 'stepping stones' pictures, to illustrate the Eightfold Path.
  Give examples of what some of the steps on the path might mean in the playground or in the family.

- **Consider** the symbols most commonly used for Buddhism – the wheel **and the lotus flower.**
  Ask: What can we learn about the beliefs of Buddhists from these symbols?

Work with 10–12 year olds

- **Examine** artefacts, pictures, video and, if possible, a vihara to find out about meditation.
  Compare meditation with pupils' own ways of being peaceful.

- **Create** collages of happiness, relating to different ages, origins and so on;
  use the collages to **explore** the limits to happiness, its impermanence.

- **Talk** about the Five Precepts.
  Ask: Would they make a perfect world? Do the pupils agree with them? Practise them? What five precepts would they offer to the world? Do they keep these themselves?

- **Think** about the opposites to the Eightfold Path and **discuss** the meaning of each of the Buddhist steps, giving examples of the behaviour that would go with them.

- **Consider** together some of the key questions that Buddhism addresses.
  Ask: Can there be an end to suffering? What is the true happiness? Where can human beings turn for refuge?

Work with 14–16 year olds

- **Examine** different ways of portraying the Buddha, and the meanings attached to them by the Buddhist community.

- **Consider** Buddhist answers to the question of suffering in discussion, debate or interviews.

- **Apply** the Buddha's 'prescription' for the ending of suffering to examples of social or personal problems.

- **Read** and **discuss** some of the Buddhist scriptures.

- **Study** the spread of Buddhism worldwide and the growing community in Britain from the viewpoints of history, sociology and religious studies.

- **Read about** or **meet** Western Buddhists.

- **Explore** Buddhist ethics as practised in the UK: for example, in prison chaplaincy or work with drug addicts.

- **Discuss** what it means to be a Buddhist and an atheist.

Christians

Christianity – a brief outline

Christianity began in the first century CE as a radical element within Judaism. It is rooted in the life and teaching of Jesus of Nazareth, a first-century Galilean Jew.

The early Jesus movements were linked strongly to Jewish life, but as the tradition spread it came to include Gentiles (those of non-Jewish background). With the conversion of the Roman Emperor Constantine in the early fourth century CE, Christianity became the official religion of the Roman Empire and spread rapidly throughout the world.

The essence (or core) of Christian belief is expressed in several creeds. There are three main creeds:

- The Apostles' Creed*
- The Nicene Creed*
- The Athanasian Creed.

The most commonly used and important

The Apostles' Creed

I believe in God, the Father Almighty,
creator of heaven and earth.

I believe in Jesus Christ, God's only Son, our Lord,
who was conceived by the Holy Spirit,
born of the Virgin Mary,
suffered under Pontius Pilate,
was crucified, died and was buried;
he descended to the dead.
On the third day he rose again;
he ascended into heaven,
he is seated at the right hand of the Father,
and he will come to judge the living and the dead.

I believe in the Holy Spirit,
the holy catholic Church,
the communion of saints,
the forgiveness of sins,
the resurrection of the body,
and the life everlasting.

Amen

Jesus

The person of Jesus is **central** to all Christian belief and worship. Jesus is both a **historical** figure, and a person of **religious** significance.

Key features in Jesus' life:

- birth and childhood
- baptism and temptations
- call of disciples and continuing relationship with them
- teaching through parables, miracles, the beatitudes and the great commandment
- Holy Week (Palm Sunday to burial)
- resurrection, ascension and second coming.

Jesus and his teachings are expressed through:

- lives of Christians through the ages and today
- worship, festivals, rituals and celebrations
- how Jesus is portrayed in the arts
- how belief in Jesus has influenced cultures and ways of life.

Denominations within Christianity

Over the course of history Christianity has broken up into a number of different churches or denominations. There are three broad groups.

- **The Orthodox Church**
  Mainly found in Eastern Europe, Russia and the Eastern Mediterranean.

- **The Roman Catholic Church**
  Found in all parts of the world, and accounting for some 60 per cent of all Christians.

- **The Protestant Churches**
  Established as a result of the Reformation, and including the Church of England, Baptists, Methodists, Salvation Army, Quakers and Presbyterians.

The Christian year

The Christian year begins with the first Sunday of Advent (the fourth Sunday before 25 December). The church has set out a cycle by which all the main events in the life of Jesus and the saints are thought about.

The most important festivals for Christians are: Easter, Pentecost and Christmas.

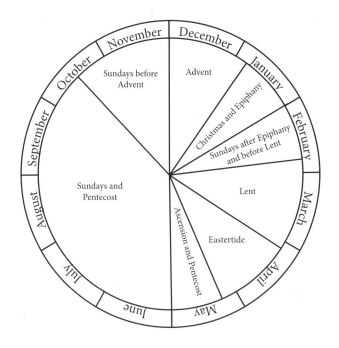

While the details of how Christians around the world celebrate these festivals may vary considerably, there are likely to be some common features:

- reading of and reflection on the festival story
- special services and acts of devotion
- symbols and artefacts
- social events within the church community.

Christians today

Christianity was introduced into Britain from continental Europe in the early years of the Common Era (CE), and is the largest and longest established of the world religions in the country.

The Christian tradition in the UK is ethnically and denominationally diverse, developing as immigrants brought with them their own distinctive traditions and expressions of faith.

Worldwide: approximately 1,999,564,000.

In Britain: approximately 38,100,000 (taking a broad view of membership).

The Bible

The Bible is a collection of 66 books. The canon (list) of books chosen for inclusion was decided in 397 CE. There are two sections:

- **The Old Testament (39 books)**
  Written over a period of some 1000 years, this section includes: laws, myths, poetry, songs, prophecies, history and stories.

- **The New Testament (27 books)**
  Covering the period from the appearance of Jesus to the deaths of Peter and Paul in 64 CE, there are four types of literature: letters (epistles), gospels, history and prophecy.

All Christians refer to the Bible and regard it as a source of authority, but within different traditions or denominations there are a variety of ways in which it is read, understood and followed.

The Apocrypha (15 writings)

Composed between 300 BCE and 100 CE, this disputed collection contains lengthy books, short letters and extracts. The writings may be included with the Old Testament, or printed as a separate section between the Old and New Testaments.

Christianity in the classroom

Christianity has a significant place in all syllabuses.

Teachers will be able to find many good classroom resources (e.g. books, posters, artefacts, DVDs, videos and websites) to support engaging, challenging and active teaching.

A balanced programme of study should include material which aims to develop understanding of:

- Jesus as a historical person and focus of faith
- Christianity as a world religion
- teaching, beliefs and practices
- festivals, rituals and practices.

The ideas on the next page suggest some activities for teachers with different age groups to plan active RE work with a focus on Christianity.

Teaching methods need to be varied and stimulating, and draw liberally on the creative and expressive arts.

Work with 6–8 year olds

- **Talk** about Jesus teaching his followers by using parables.
  Ask: What is Jesus' story?

- **Read** some of Jesus' parables.
  Use dance and drama to explore the meanings of Jesus' parables.

- **Visit** a church; talk with the vicar, minister or priest.
  Use these resources to explore the symbolism of artefacts. Create class guides to the local church.

- **Learn** about the Bible.
  Ask: How did the Bible come into being? How is the Bible understood and used by Christians in different times and places?

- **Join in** a simulation of a Christian festival or ceremony.
  Ask: What happens, when and why? Talk about feelings when joining in such celebrations.

Work with 10–12 year olds

- **Recognise** key symbols in Christian art, worship and language.
  Ask: How have Christians expressed their beliefs through the creative and expressive arts?

- **Compare** Christian places of worship.
  Ask: What is their significance in the lives of believers? What places are special to me? How do I show that they are special?

- **Read** about Jesus performing miracles.
  Ask: What makes something miraculous? Create a TV programme, including interviews with eyewitnesses.

- **Explore** the multicultural nature of Christianity, and its various denominations and traditions.
  Ask: How is this diversity reflected in the community where I live? In what ways will this affect me as I grow up?

Work with 14–16 year olds

- **Debate** the extent of the impact of Jesus Christ on history, and on the current structure of Western society. To what extent has this impact been positive?

- **Explore** the concept of 'church' as outlined by Saint Paul.
  Discuss how 'church' today is understood and experienced within different denominations or traditions.

- **Interview** some practising Christians.
  Identify and **write about** the ways in which faith affects the way Christians live their lives today.

- **Discuss** and **evaluate** the extent to which contemporary culture in the UK is affecting the practice of Christianity. What are the implications for values in the lives of individual Christians?

- **Research** liberation theology and **evaluate** how far this approach to Christianity fits the character and teaching of Jesus. Was Jesus a liberation theologian?

- **Identify** the Bible passages that refer to the Christian belief in life after death.
  Reflect on your own beliefs.
  Design a piece of artwork to depict your feelings about life after death.

Hindus

Hinduism – a brief outline

Hinduism dates back to around 1800 BCE, and has no single founder. The word 'Hindu' is related to a Sanskrit word, *Sindhu*, which is the name for the river known as the Indus in English.

Hinduism is often called **Dharma** or the **Sanatan Dharma** (eternal way) by those who practise it.

The Hindu tradition is ancient in origin, diverse, inclusive and ever-changing. It may help in understanding the Hindu way to think of it as a huge river, with many streams flowing into it, flowing into a delta of many waterways flowing into the sea.

As in other religions, diversity plays a major part within Hinduism. Therefore, beliefs and practices vary according to:

- historical streams
- geographical location
- cultural traditions.

Similarly, there is a wide range of schools of thought, philosophical positions, religious practices and foci for devotion that are accepted.

However, within this diversity there are a number of beliefs and practices that are more commonly accepted, for example the authority of the **Vedas** (sacred texts).

The Hindu way

The Hindu way has four aims (*punusharthas*):

- **dharma** (religious or moral duty)
- **artha** (economic development, providing for family and society by honest means)
- **kama** (regulated enjoyment of the pleasures and beauty of life)
- **moksha** (liberation from the round of birth and rebirth).

A Hindu is true to his or her *dharma* if all appropriate religious and moral duties are carried out.

Hindu beliefs

- **Dharma**

  The key concept of **dharma**, which sums up ideas about a person's social and religious duty, cannot be easily translated by a single English word, but it introduces other key terms in the Hindu vision of what it means to be human.

- **Brahman**

  Everything comes from **Brahman**, and ultimately returns to Brahman. **The One** is unknowable, and unapproachable, but human beings can come to God through the many forms of gods and goddesses.

- **Atman**

  The Hindu concept of the human self, or **atman**, is important. The atman is the self (soul), that which pervades all things and which does not die.

- **Karma**

  The atman returns to the earth in another body according to the law of **karma**, or cause and effect. Karma is the total effect of one's actions, good and bad. All actions have their consequences.

- **Samsara**

  This cycle of reincarnation (**samsara**) sends the atman to live a duty or dharma in many lives in the search for liberation (**moksha**).

Dharma varies according to birth, and the circumstances of life, but the Hindu way values harmlessness to all living creatures and devotion to the divine and other people.

These values are expressed through, for example:

- a vegetarian diet
- a commitment to non-violence
- a close family structure
- a way of life that makes time for worship and meditation.

Community, traditions and worship

The family community is an important focus for faith among Hindus.

Respect for older members of the family, a sense of belonging to a wider family and **caste** or **jati**, the tradition of marking stages of life by rituals, and progressing in devotion or faith towards renunciation of earthly life, all combine to enrich Hindu community life.

It is in the **family** that the long tradition of worship, community and values is shared with each generation – often chiefly by mothers and wives – made alive in practice, and drawn upon for strength, security, peace and purpose.

Festivals typically draw family and community together, for example:

- **Shivaratri** (February/March)
- **Holi** (February/March)
- **Rama Navami** (March/April)
- **Janmashtami** (August/September)
- **Navaratri** (September/October)
- **Divali** or **Deepawali** (October/November)

Hinduism today

The origins of the Sanatan Dharma are in ancient India, yet its contemporary expressions are to be found all over the world, in Africa, the Caribbean and Europe as well as in Asia.

The largest Hindu communities in the UK are in Greater London, Birmingham, Coventry and Leicester, and there are some 130 Hindu places of worship.

It is thought that 55–70 per cent of Hindus in the UK are of Gujurati origin, and 15–20 of Punjabi origin. Wherever they are living, it is usual for Hindus to maintain links with their ancestral region and to speak their ancestral language among themselves.

It is very difficult to be accurate about the numbers of people who are Hindu, but responsible estimates suggest:

Worldwide: in the region of 811,336,000, the vast majority living in India.

In Britain: at least 400,000.

Sacred texts

Hindu faith is rooted in scriptures. A number of sacred texts, some revealed and some remembered (called **sruti** and **smrti** respectively), each have an important place.

The widest authority is attributed to the Vedas. The range of scriptures includes:

- social and ethical laws
- philosophical material
- hymns
- epic stories of the gods and goddesses
- poetry.

The use, discussion and interpretation of these scriptures enliven the Hindu community. For example, the **Bhagavad Gita**, a part of the epic **Mahabharata**, is often found in Hindu homes, wrapped in silk, read, learned and recited, and used as a source of guidance in life.

Hinduism in the classroom

It is appropriate for pupils of any school age to study Hinduism. Many syllabuses require this, and others make it optional.

There is no shortage of good quality curriculum materials for all key stages (e.g. books, posters, artefacts, DVDs, videos and websites); many of the best of these include Hindu authors.

A balanced programme of study should include opportunities for pupils to think about:

- festivals
- worship
- stories from sacred texts
- pilgrimage
- the importance of the concepts and values that inspire the Hindu community.

Teaching methods need to be varied and stimulating, with an emphasis on the creative and expressive arts.

Work with 6–8 year olds

- **Listen** to stories about Hindu children in Britain today, and about Hindu gods, goddesses and heroes.

- **Plan** the sharing of a dramatic version of a Hindu story to **present** to older children.

- **Talk** about the oldest and wisest stories and sayings they know, and ask parents and other adults to tell them such stories and sayings.

- **Practise** greetings (e.g. hello, bonjour, namaste, peace be with you) and associated hand gestures. **Learn** that the Hindu greeting 'Namaste' means 'the divine spark in me greets the spark of God in you'.

- **Use** artefacts to see how all five senses are in use when a Hindu worships.

Work with 10–12 year olds

- **Use** the creative and expressive arts as 'windows' into Hindu ideas about life. Examples could include **exploring** stories through dance, and the use of the symbolism of colour.

- **Visit** a Hindu place of worship (or receive a Hindu visitor to school) and take part in a question and answer session on Hindu ways of life.

- **Use** Hindu artefacts, particularly *murtis* of the gods and goddesses, along with Hindu stories, to **explore** symbols of the powers and attributes of the divine.

- **Make** pictorial charts of the life cycle, and **think** about both the rituals and the beliefs associated with our passing lives.

- **Explore** Hindu ideas about the knowledge and mystery of the divine, using creative strategies.

Work with 14–16 year olds

- **Consider** key Hindu ideas of Brahman, atman, dharma, karma, reincarnation and moksha. **Devise** diagrams to show how these ideas fit together.

- **Examine** the contours of the Hindu community in Britain, with reference to the diversity and flexibility of the tradition.

- **Explore** Hindu commitments to non-violence, harmlessness and vegetarian food. **Contrast** this with some Western attitudes. Reflect the example and teaching of major religious teachers in your response.

- **Ask** questions about the nature of the 'self', about what it means to be human. **Explore** Hindu answers to these questions.

- **Consider** the role of festivals within Hindu tradition, and the myths used at these times. How effective can these occasions be as a focus and prompt for personal reflection?

- **Investigate** the presence of Hinduism in the media (TV, radio, film, magazines, newspapers and the internet). **Consider** the advantages and disadvantages of religious events, stories and sacred writings being presented in these ways.

Jews

Judaism – a brief outline

Judaism is the oldest of the monotheistic religions, dating back to the time of Abraham (approximately 1900 BCE). He was called into a covenant with God to start a people that God described as numbering as many as the dust of the earth and the stars in the sky.

Jews believe in one God, the creator, beyond space and time, yet a personal God, interested in humanity, and intimately involved with the world, caring for and loving creation.

Three areas of fundamental importance in Judaism are:

- **God**
- the **Torah**
- the **people and the land.**

God

Jews believe in one creator God who cares for all people. Jews worship God, saying blessings and thanks, and believe that God has chosen them to be the people of Israel.

Central to Jewish belief is the **Shema,** which begins with the words: 'Hear, O Israel: The LORD our God is one LORD; and you shall love the LORD your God with all your heart, and with all your soul, and with all your might' (Deuteronomy 6: 4-5).

The Shema is written on parchment inside a **mezuzah** and attached to the doorposts of Jewish homes; to be remembered each time it is passed. It is also placed inside **tefillin,** and strapped by some Jews to their forehead and left arm for prayer.

Yom Kippur, the Day of Atonement, is a very holy day when Jews fast and spend time repenting of their sins, restoring their relationship with God and with each other, giving them an opportunity to get closer to God.

The Torah

The **Torah** (meaning teaching, instruction or law) is extremely important to Jews. The term is used in a narrow sense to mean the first five books of the Hebrew Bible (Genesis, Exodus, Leviticus, Numbers and Deuteronomy) and in a wider sense to include the whole of the Hebrew Bible and the Talmud (see below).

At its heart is the message revealed to Moses for the Jewish people on Mount Sinai in the desert. It includes 613 **Mitzvot** (laws), of which 365 are negative commandments, outlining what Jews should not do, and 248 positive things, which Jews should do.

The whole Torah includes:

- the **TeNaKh,** or 'Written Torah', or Hebrew Bible, consisting of: the **Pentateuch** (Torah), the **Prophets** (Nevi'im) and the **Writings** (Ketuvim)
- the **Talmud,** or Oral Law, which is made up of the **Mishnah** (the first writing down of the oral tradition, about 200 CE) and the **Gemara** (a commentary on the Mishnah)

Jews regularly study the Torah: to do so is to worship God.

The Torah is held in great esteem and kept in a special place in the synagogue called the **Ark.** A weekly portion is read aloud in the Shabbat synagogue service and there is an annual cycle of readings including all five books of the Torah.

Simchat Torah ('rejoicing in the Torah') celebrates the completion of the annual reading of the Torah. It is a joyous festival, held on the 23rd of the Jewish month of Tishrei. Torah scrolls are taken from the Ark and carried or danced around the synagogue seven times. The concluding section of Deuteronomy is read, and, immediately following, the opening section of Genesis (B'reishit) is read.

The people and the land

Judaism teaches that people are made in God's image, and the family and home are very important. **Shabbat** is celebrated at home on a Friday evening after dusk by a family meal, followed by a time of rest set aside to worship God and spend time together as a family.

Kashrut is the body of Jewish law dealing with the foods that are 'fit' to be eaten. These food laws go back more than 3,000 years to the time when God gave the Torah to Moses, and continue to play an important part in the daily lives of many Jews.

Food which meets the demands of kashrut is called **kosher.** 'Keeping kosher' involves eating only certain animals which have been killed in a special way. Meat and milk products must not be mixed; separate sets of kitchen utensils are used for these two types of food. Food which is forbidden is **treyfah** (or **treif**).

The **land of Israel** is also very important. Although Jews live all over the world, Israel has always been a very special place. Jews believe that this is the land promised to Abraham and his descendants, and that God led them to settle there. Later, King David established the kingdom of Israel with Jerusalem as its capital. A part of the western wall of the second temple in Jerusalem is visited by pilgrim Jews.

Jews today

Jews have long been associated with the UK, with the first Jewish settlers coming after the Norman conquest.

The UK Jewish population consists of both **Sephardi** (originally from Spain, Portugal and the Middle East) and **Ashkenazi** Jews (of central and east European origin), with Ashkenazi Jews being the larger group.

The largest Jewish communities are found in the Greater London area, Manchester, Leeds and Glasgow. There are also Jewish communities in Birmingham, Bournemouth, Brighton, Gateshead, Liverpool and Southend.

Worldwide: approximately 14,434,000.

In Britain: approximately 283,000

Schools within Judaism

There are two main schools within Judaism: orthodox and progressive. Both believe in the importance of the Torah, but they place difference emphases on it.

- **Orthodox Jews** believe that both the Torah and the oral law contained in the Talmud have been revealed by God and as such contain God's unchanging words.

  Hasidic Jews come within the tradition of orthodoxy. They follow the teachings of Israel ben Eliezer, also known as Baal Shem Tov, who took a mystical approach to Judaism.

- **Progressive Jews** (which includes Jews of both the Liberal and Reform traditions) believe that the Torah was inspired by God, but written down by human beings according to God's will. Therefore they may believe that God's law can be reinterpreted, and the laws brought up to date for today.

- **Masorti (Conservative) Jews** emerged as a group at the beginning of the twentieth century. They may be thought of as halfway between Orthodox and Progressive Judaism. Masorti Jews aim to comply with as much of the Torah as is practicable in modern society, but may compromise in certain respects (e.g. by driving to synagogue on the Sabbath).

Judaism in the classroom

It is appropriate for pupils of any school age to study Judaism. Many syllabuses require this, and others make it optional. When a syllabus gives choices, Judaism is sometimes chosen because of its close links with Christianity.

However, to share resources with Christianity and to base work solely on 'Old Testament' stories does not do justice to Judaism. It must be studied as a living faith in its own right, not as the roots of Christianity.

The ideas on the next page suggest some activities for teachers with different age groups to plan active RE work with a focus on Judaism. They are intended to be used flexibly, and to draw upon the wide range of resources available on Judaism.

Work with 6–8 year olds

- **Lay** a Friday night Shabbat table.
  Ask: What is the significance of each of the artefacts used?

- **Make** a spice box with household spices, and **illustrate** on the lid what pupils found most interesting about Shabbat.

- **Read and enact** the story behind the festival of Purim or Hanukkah.
  Ask: What do the stories reveal about the nature of God?

- **Talk about** the words and meaning of the Ten Commandments for Jews. Write and draw how they think people should behave towards others (and God if they wish).

- **Learn** about the Shema, and **write** a letter to remind Jews they should love and worship God.

- **Invite** a Jewish visitor into school.
  Prepare and **ask** questions about what being Jewish means in everyday life.

Work with 10–12 year olds

- **Research** Jewish food and Shabbat laws and **plan** kosher menus for weekday and Shabbat meals.
  Ask: What is the significance of keeping kosher for Jews?

- **Compare** public and family **worship.**
  Ask: Why do pupils think family worship is so important to Jews?

- **Design** a mystery activity based on the Exodus and the need for the Ten Commandments, focusing on the need for rules in all societies.
  Ask: What would be the implications if the Decalogue was obeyed by all?

- **Design** a holiday brochure for non-Jewish visitors to Israel in which the following **questions** are addressed: What is the importance for Jews of visiting Jewish holy sites in Israel and Jerusalem? How might such a visit be different for non-Jews?

- **Find out** all the objects that Jews might have in their homes which identify them as being Jewish.
  Ask: What is the symbolism and significance of each?

Work with 14–16 year olds

- **Compare** the ideas about God presented by Exodus, and by the scholar Maimonides.
  Consider how such contrasting ideas about God might be helpful.
  Reflect on your own ideas and questions about God.

- **Compare** the practices of Orthodox and Progressive Judaism.
  Discuss: How important are change, continuity and growth within the history of Judaism?

- **Analyse** the events which resulted in the Shoah (Holocaust).
  Examine the factors which result in racism and prejudice.
  Suggest how society could best deal with these issues, and include Jewish responses.

- **Consider** the part the concept of nationhood has played in the life of Jews.
  Debate: How far is it possible to separate religion from nationality?

Muslims

Islam – a brief outline

The religion of Islam was revealed to the Prophet Muhammad in the seventh century CE. The word Islam means submission or surrender; the life of a Muslim is spent, therefore, submitting to **Allah** (God).

Muhammad (570–632 CE) was born in the Arabian city of Makkah where, from the age of 40, he received a series of revelations from Allah. The revelations were received over a period of 23 years, and were delivered by the Angel Jibril (Gabriel). These revelations form the **Qur'an**, the sacred text of Islam.

Muslims do not believe that Muhammad brought a new faith. Rather, he is seen as the last of a long line of prophets sent by God to guide people on to the right path. Jesus (Isa) was one such prophet. Muhammad is regarded by Muslims as the **'seal of the prophets'**. Muslims often follow the Prophet's name with the words 'peace be upon him' (pbuh) as a mark of respect.

Those who accept Muhammad as the 'seal of the prophets' and his revelations as being from Allah, were welcomed into the Muslim community (**ummah**). This community migrated from Makkah to Madinah in 622 CE (the **hijrah**), a formative event in the history of Islam.

The Muslim way

Muslims regard Islam as a complete way of life (**din**). There are four main concepts within Islam which underpin all Muslim belief and behaviour:

- **tawhid**
- **iman**
- **ibadah**
- **akhlaq**

The **five pillars** provide a structure for the daily spiritual life of the Muslim.

Tawhid

Tawhid is the oneness of Allah. Islam teaches an absolute monotheism. To regard anyone or anything as being equal to Allah, or even a partner with Allah, is described as **shirk** and is absolutely forbidden. The Muslim profession of faith, the **Shahadah**, declares: 'There is no god except Allah.' This is not just an abstract theological statement but one which is worked out in many ways. God cannot be represented, but the geometrical designs so prominent in Islamic culture are a reflection of the unity and beauty of Allah. And if God is one, the human race is one.

Iman

Iman is faith, the believer's response to God. Faith is expressed primarily in acceptance of Muhammad as the final messenger of God and of the **Qur'an** as the revealed word of God. Qur'an means 'reciting' and is the definitive guide for all Muslims. The Shahadah continues: 'There is no god except Allah; Muhammad is the messenger of Allah.'

Ibadah

Muslims use this single word for both **worship** and any **action** that is performed with the intention of obeying Allah. This worship and belief-in-action are inextricably linked by the very language. This concept covers many of the most obvious features of Islam, including prayer, fasting, pilgrimage and charitable giving. As the whole of life is worship, no special emphasis is placed on any one aspect of obligation. The five pillars provide a structure for the daily spiritual life of a Muslim.

Akhlaq

Akhlaq is a term which cannot be translated by a single English equivalent. It means both behaviour and the attitudes and social ethical codes which lie behind specific forms of behaviour. Under this heading are included aspects of family and social life and also issues for the whole of humanity, for example, the possibility of an Islamic social and economic order which is a viable alternative to both capitalism and communism.

The five pillars

- **Shahadah**

  The declaration of faith

- **Salat**

  Ritual prayer carried out five times a day

- **Zakat**

  A welfare due, usually 2.5 per cent of income

- **Sawm**

  A month of fasting (Ramadan) and spiritual discipline

- **Hajj**

  Pilgrimage to Makkah.

Schools within Islam

There are two main schools within Islam.

- **Sunni Muslims** (from sunnat, meaning tradition) believe that they alone hold to the true faith as revealed to Muhammad. They maintain that leadership can only pass to a member of Muhammad's tribe (the Quraysh). Up to 90 per cent of Muslims are Sunnis.

- **Shi'ah Muslims** maintain that leadership should only pass to the descendants of Ali (the cousin and son-in-law of Muhammad). Shi'ah means 'the party of Ali'. Shi'ah Muslims live mainly in Iraq, Lebanon, Iran and India.

Muslims today

From its origins in Arabia, Islam has spread to the Indian subcontinent, Africa, Malaysia, Indonesia, the Philippines and Europe.

Muslims have lived in the UK since the early nineteenth century. The largest Muslim communities are found in the West Midlands, Lancashire, West Yorkshire, Greater London and Central Scotland. Most major towns and cities have a sizeable Muslim population.

Worldwide: approximately 1,118,243,000.

In Britain: between 1,000,000 and 1,500,000.

The Qur'an and Hadith

The Qur'an (that which is read or recited) is regarded as the actual 'word of God', as revealed to Muhammad. It gives guidance on all aspects of a Muslim's faith and behaviour, and covers a range of everyday topics.

The Qur'an has 114 chapters (**surahs**) which are usually known by their titles rather than their numbers. Each chapter is divided into units or verses (**ayahs**).

The Hadith (meaning **narrative** or **report**) is second in importance to the Qur'an. It contains records of the actions (**Sunnah**) and words of the Prophet Muhammad and his closest friends. There are two broad types:

- **Prophetic Hadith** (the words and sayings of Muhammad himself)

- **Sacred Hadith** (their authority goes back through the Prophet to Allah himself; they were revealed but not included in the Qur'an).

Islam in the classroom

It is appropriate for pupils of any school age to study Islam. Many syllabuses require this, and others make it optional.

Teachers will be able to find a wide range of quality resources (e.g. books, posters, artefacts, DVDs, videos and websites) for the engaging, challenging and active teaching of Islam.

A balanced programme of study should include material that aims to develop understanding of:

- Muhammad

- teaching, beliefs and values

- sources of authority: Qur'an and Hadith

- festivals, rituals and practices

- Muslims in Britain today.

The ideas on the next page suggest some activities for teachers with different age groups to plan active RE work with a focus on Islam. They are intended to be used flexibly.

Work with 6–8 year olds

- **Listen** to stories about the life of Muhammad.
  Ask: What do you think is special about Muhammad for Muslims?

- **Join in** a simulation of a Muslim festival or ceremony. What happens, when and why?
  Talk about feelings when joining in such celebrations.

- **Talk** about how Muslims celebrate family life and the birth of a baby.
  Ask: What is special about belonging?

- **Watch** a video about hajj. Think about the ways in which hajj reminds Muslims that all people are of equal value.
  Ask: How might the world today be different if everybody believed this? Why do people find it hard to treat people equally?

- **Explore** the concept of special journeys.
  Ask: what is their significance for believers?

Work with 10–12 year olds

- **Relate** the story of the revelation of the Qur'an to Muhammad.
  Ask: Whom do pupils turn to for guidance? What books are special to them? How is the Qur'an used in the life of a Muslim?

- **Talk** about the Shahadah ('There is no god except Allah') and use the ninety-nine names of Allah to **explore** his attributes.

- **Focus** on the Muslim daily prayers (salah) as a time which Muslims set aside for the worship of Allah.
  Ask: What do pupils consider sufficiently important to set aside time for?

- **Explore** Islamic art looking at shape, pattern and colour.
  Ask: what is their significance for Muslims, in the context of tawhid.

Work with 14–16 year olds

- **Consider** the implications of one God, one creation, one human race (tawhid). Can a Muslim be a racist or belong to an organisation like the National Front?

- **Reflect:** Iman is a Muslim's response in faith to Allah's revelation to Muhammad. What faith do pupils have? Who do they believe?

- **Discuss:** Ibadah is a response to Allah in worship and in daily living. How does this affect Muslim values and choices?

- **Consider** the concept of a society based on a religious code.
  Debate: What are the implications for individuals within an Islamic social and economic order?

- **Research** the role of women and men within Islam, and the importance of family life.
  Evaluate the extent to which Muhammad can be considered a champion of equal rights.

Sikhs

Sikhism – a brief outline

Guru Nanak, the first of the ten Sikh gurus, lived in the Punjab region of India over 500 years ago. When he was about 30 years old, he received the call to preach the Word of God, and travelled extensively to fulfil this mission. Sikhism is seen as an original, revealed religion.

The **Ten Gurus** each contributed something to the developing faith and way of life that is the **Sikh Dharam**.

The Gurus

- Guru Nanak (1469–1539)
- Guru Angad (1504–1552)
- Guru Amar Das (1479–1574)
- Guru Ram Das (1534–1581)
- Guru Arjan (1563–1606)
- Guru Hargobind (1595–1644)]
- Guru Har Rai (1631–1661)
- Guru Har Krishan (1656–1664)
- Guru Tegh Bahadur (1622–1675)
- Guru Gobind Singh (1666–1708)

Guru Gobind Singh, the tenth Guru, founded the Sikh **Khalsa** at Baisakhi just over 300 years ago (April 1699 CE). It was on this occasion that he encouraged his followers to wear what are now known as the **five Ks**.

He also declared that the line of human gurus was to come to an end with him, and that the Sikh Scriptures were to be their living Guru.

The Guru's teaching, now focused through the **Guru Granth Sahib**, emphasises belief in one God and the worship of the same, universal love, peace and equality, and the importance of service (**sewa**). Like Muslims, Sikhs believe on one God and, like Hindus, they believe in the cycle of birth, death and rebirth.

Sikh practices

Sikh practice includes:

- **using stories** from the Gurus' lives as examples of how to put faith into practice.
- **paying attention** to the Gurus' teaching and reciting the Guru Granth Sahib.
- **celebrating festivals:**
  - **gurpurbs,** which are held in honour of one of the ten Gurus, to celebrate their life or death (e.g. the birthdays of Guru Nanak and Guru Gobind Singh, and the martyrdoms of Guru Arjan and Guru Tegh Bahadur). Other anniversaries are also gurpurbs (e.g. the installation of the Adi Granth in 1604 CE).
  - **melas**, which coincide with important Hindu festivals, but on which something important happened during the lives of one of the Gurus (e.g. Divali, when Guru Hargobind was freed from captivity and insisted on taking with him all other captives).
- **rituals** for:
  - naming
  - turban-tying
  - amrit
  - marriage
  - death.

The Sikh community

Sikh community is reinforced by:

- the Sikh symbol, the **Khanda**
- the **Khalsa**, or brotherhood of Amrit Sikhs
- the wearing of the **five Ks** by some Sikhs
- worship in the **gurdwara** and sharing in the **langar**
- visiting the **Golden Temple** (Harimandir) at Amritsar.

The Guru Granth Sahib

The scriptures were first compiled by **Guru Arjan**, the fifth Guru. He ordered that all the texts be brought to him. He corrected some, rejected others which were not by the Gurus and which did not contain the Sikh message, and added some songs and hymns. This task took over a year, and was completed in 1604 CE.

Guru Arjan's collection is called the **Adi Granth**, meaning 'first collection'.

Guru Gobind Singh revised the Adi Granth, adding the teaching of the ten Gurus along with those of other holy men. In this book, the **Guru Granth Sahib**, he told his followers they would find all the guidance and inspiration they needed to live out their lives as Sikhs.

All Sikh ceremonies and services take place in the presence of the Guru Granth Sahib, which is treated with the greatest respect and honour.

The gurdwara

The gurdwara, the home of the Guru, is a place of worship, housing the Guru Granth Sahib. This may be in someone's home, providing that they can care correctly for it. However, a gurdwara is usually a separate building that is not only for worship but a focus for the life of the Sikh community.

In the gurdwara, the Sikh idea of equality is practised: anyone can participate in worship; no one is excluded; leading worship is open to all who can read the scriptures; all eat together in the langar (a free community kitchen).

Sikhs today

The first British gurdwara was opened in Shepherd's Bush in 1911 and there are now over 200 gurdwaras around the UK.

There are substantial Sikh populations in Greater London (especially Southall), Birmingham, Coventry, Leicester, Wolverhampton, Bradford, Cardiff and Glasgow.

Worldwide: more than 23,000,000 (mainly in the Punjab).

In Britain: more than 350,000 (the largest Sikh community outside the Punjab).

Sikh beliefs, values and ethics

There is one God:

- The supreme truth, creator and eternal (see the **Mool Mantar**).

Human beings can find value in:

- Remembering and meditating on the name of God (**Sat Nam**)
- Honest work (**Kirat Karna**)
- Charitable giving (**Vand Chhakna**)
- Service to others (**Sewa**).

Ethical decisions are informed by:

- The principle of **equality**
- **Sewa** (This 'selfless service' is the outworking of the worship of God who is everywhere and in everyone).

The use of any sort of **intoxicating drug** (alcohol, tobacco and illicit drugs) is forbidden to Amrit Sikhs. **Family life** is very important – **adultery** is thoroughly condemned and **divorce** is frowned upon. **Respect for and valuing** life is important since life comes from God.

Sikhism in the classroom

The study of Sikhism is appropriate for pupils of any school age. Many syllabuses require this, and others make it optional.

There are many sources of good resource material (e.g. books, posters, artefacts, DVDs, videos and websites) to support engaging, challenging and active teaching. A balanced programme of study should include material about:

- the Gurus
- Sikh beliefs and values
- the gurdwara and community life
- festivals, rituals and practices
- Sikhs in Britain today

The suggestions on the next page are designed to help teachers with different age groups to plan active RE work with a focus on Sikhism. They are intended to be used flexibly.

Work with 6–8 year olds

- **Listen** to stories about the Gurus' lives or about Sikh children in Britain today and **respond** with questions and ideas. **Make** a 'zigzag' book with appropriate text and illustrations.

- **Join in** a simulation of a Sikh festival or ceremony. What happens, when and why? **Talk** about feelings when joining in such celebrations.

- **Look** carefully at artefacts like the Khanda. **Learn** about their symbolism and significance.

- **Think** about the idea that all people are of equal value. **Ask:** Is this happening in the world today? How can we help make the world a more equal place?

- **Make** a picture of a Sikh flag. **Talk** about its symbolism.

Work with 10–12 year olds

- **Retell** stories of the Gurus in various visual, dramatic or written forms – focus on what Sikhs learn from such stories. **Ask:** What can I learn from them?

- **Make** collages on the theme of difference and equality. **Think** about the impact of Sikh teaching about equality on the way people in this country (or town, school, class) treat others. **Ask:** What would Guru Nanak say if he took our assembly?

- **Talk** about different Sikh names for God; explore ideas about God in other faiths and the pupils' own ideas. **Conduct** a survey about belief in God.

- **Make** booklets to illustrate a guided tour round a gurdwara, or a visit to Amritsar and the Harimandir (Golden Temple)

- **Examine** artefacts such as the five Ks and those associated with Amrit, and **write** about the value of these to Sikhs. **Talk** about what it means to belong and the symbols of belonging which pupils in the class have or use.

Work with 14–16 year olds

- **Consider** the questions of Sikh identity in modern British culture, from religious and sociological perspectives.

- **Examine** the story of Guru Nanak's disappearance and revelation of the divine, and **consider** Sikh interpretations of it. **Discuss** the meaning of 'God' and consider philosophical issues arising from it.

- **Devise** plans for a new, purpose-built gurdwara in the locality.

- **Read about** and **meet** British Sikhs.

- **Devise** various ethical and moral dilemmas. **Explore** how Sikhs might respond, putting the teaching of the Gurus into practice.

Non-religious ethical life stances

Religious Education is not just for the religious, but for all pupils. Most pupils in schools in Britain today do not identify very closely, if at all, with a religious community, and so it is appropriate that RE should include consideration of some of the alternatives to religion that exist in our society. The myth that only religious people take ethics seriously is all too common; in fact there are various philosophies and approaches to life which have nothing to do with any particular religion, but call followers to lives of love and unselfishness.

These living belief systems can be grouped together as 'non-religious ethical life stances'. Their forms are often eclectic, but include everything from rationalist atheism and agnosticism, through post-Marxist accounts of humanity, to deliberately 'dis-traditioned' postmodern spiritualities or life stances.

People who feel at home with such descriptions do not all identify formally with humanism, but the British Humanist Association is perhaps the most visible and organised non-religious ethical life stance to be seen in the nation's public life.

If the RE field of enquiry includes an exploration of the experience we share as human beings, and an opportunity for a pupil to take a personal search further, it follows that teachers can plan to consider beliefs, values, celebrations and ideas from ethical traditions such as humanism.

An ancient tradition

Humanism has a long history, and many great intellectuals from past centuries have influenced the modern humanist tradition. These figures would include thinkers from classical civilisation such as Epicurus and Seneca, as well as enlightenment philosophers from Thomas Paine through John Stuart Mill to Bertrand Russell.

Contemporary humanists in the UK include such public figures as Claire Rayner, George Mellor and Professor Bernard Crick.

A community dimension

Though relatively few humanists belong to a humanist organisation (the British Humanist Association has about 4000 members), the ideas of humanism are very influential in the UK today, and many people recognise themselves when they hear humanism described.

Humanism briefly described

Humanists are people who:

- believe primarily in humanity

- hold that human nature is a remarkable product of the universe, but not the product of any divine creation, and that the human race can expect no help from the gods

- place their confidence in the power of human reason, goodwill and science to solve the problems that face us, and reject the power of prayer or worship

- accept the limitations of a lifetime and notice that we live on in the memories of others and in our achievements, but reject all ideas of rebirth, resurrection or eternal life

- when it comes to ethics, believe that their own reasoned sense of goodness and happiness should guide them to decide what is right for themselves and others

- are often concerned for the greatest happiness for the greatest number

- think it is best to make ethical decisions by looking at the individual case, not just by applying a hard and fast rule

- have often been active in working for human rights, and get involved in a variety of social and ethical issues.

'I prefer to say that the spiritual elements which are usually styled divine are part and parcel of human nature.'

Sir Julian Huxley, FRS

Those who identify themselves as humanist may have special secular welcomes for a new baby, wedding ceremonies based on humanist ideals and non-religious funerals. They may celebrate festivals in a secular way, whether this means joining in New Year celebrations with relish, or marking United Nations Day.

Humanism and ethics

Ethically, humanism is often personal and individual, liberal, tolerant and rationally based. Humanists may be in favour of free choice in matters such as euthanasia or divorce, and may emphasise virtues such as truthfulness, generosity, democracy, tolerance, justice and co-operation. Humanists try to put the **'golden rule'** into action: treat other people as you would like them to treat you.

Examples

There are relatively few published resources that deal explicitly with Humanism, particularly for the primary phase. On the right there are two examples which might be useful.

Non-religious traditions in the classroom

As RE explores human experience, beliefs and values, the non-religious approaches to life will be relevant at many points. This is reflected in the QCA's non-statutory National Framework for RE (2004) which specifies for each key stage that 'a secular world view, where appropriate' is a desirable area of study (3d).

Teachers can confidently include this material in the RE curriculum wherever it makes a contribution to the aims of RE as expressed in their statutory curriculum documentation, e.g. locally agreed syllabus or diocesan guidelines.

A balanced study of humanism should include:

- exploration of humanist beliefs and values

- learning about some key historical and contemporary humanist figures

- finding out about humanist activities and ceremonies

Teaching methods need to be varied, challenging and stimulating.

With an approach to life based on humanity and reason, humanists recognise that moral choices are properly founded on human nature and experience alone. We value the truth, and consider facts as well as feelings in reaching a judgement. Humanists reject the idea of any supernatural agency intervening to help or hinder us.

British Humanist Association

Ten non-commandments

1. Never accept authority.

2. Base your conduct on simple, humane principles.

3. Strive to eliminate poverty.

4. Strive to eliminate war.

5. Do not be a snob.

6. In sexual behaviour, use your brains as well as your genitals, and always in that order.

7. Take the care necessary to enjoy family life and marriage.

8. Keep the law.

9. Commit yourself to active citizenship.

10. Have confidence in the modern world and your powers to improve it.

In 1964 the humanist Ronald Fletcher published a pamphlet called *The Ten Non-Commandments: A Humanist Decalogue*. **The text illustrates** the spirit and feel of humanism rather well, though, like other such texts, it requires a lot of unpacking and interpretation. It carries none of the authority of sacred texts in religious traditions, but the humanists would be proud of that. **It is suitable for the learning needs of pupils from about age 12.**

Five humanist slogans

One local group of humanists in Bromley has produced a set of posters to promote humanist ideas. They have the following slogans on them:

Good without God

Morals without religion

Rites without religion

Ceremonies without superstition

Ethical atheism

Work with 6–8 year olds

- **Look** at the humanist symbol of the Happy Human.
  Talk about what makes people happy and sad. Focus (perhaps through role-play) on the ways people can help and support those who have had sadness in their lives. Collage or artwork might be produced.

- **Listen** to, and **talk** about, stories which exemplify human goodness without reference to any god.

- **Plan** and **participate in** celebrations of the work of 'secular' organisations which challenge injustice, care for the environment or guard human rights.

- 'Do to others as you would like them to do to you.' **Draw** cartoons to illustrate the 'golden rule' when it works and when it doesn't.

- **Compare** a 'secular' celebration like New Year or a birthday with a religious one.
  Ask: What is the same, and what is different?

Work with 10–12 year olds

- **Learn to use** the terms 'agnostic', 'atheist', 'secular' and 'non-religious' in speaking about issues of meaning, purpose and ethics in any RE context.

- 'Do to others as you would like them to do to you.' **Compare** versions of this rule found in many different contexts.
  Apply it to some moral problems.
  Illustrate how 'morality without God' can use this idea.

- **Examine** the ways humanists celebrate key steps through life
  Explore similarities and differences compared with religious ceremonies.

- **Use** the five humanist slogans on page 84 to get pupils to **think** about meanings, symbol and visual expression.
  Ask them to **design** posters that illustrate the slogans, using non-religious symbolism and natural images.

- **Discuss, argue** or **debate** the reasons that humanists hold to support their rejection of religious ideas like God, prayer, revelation or life after death.

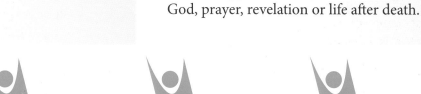

Work with 14–16 year olds

- **Research** the ways key figures in humanism have put their ideas into action. Examples could include Thomas Paine, Simone de Beauvoir or Bertrand Russell.

- **Study** the 'Humanist Decalogue' (Fletcher) given on page 84.
  Compare it to some other codes for living, and ask: What if everyone lived like this? What kinds of families, schools, communities would we get?

- **Analyse** humanist ethical ideas and reasoning about issues such as sexuality, euthanasia or world poverty, and **articulate their own positions** on these issues.

- **Apply** Ninian Smart's seven dimensions of religion to humanism and analyse the question: 'Is humanism a religion?'
  Ask: Does humanism have social, ethical, doctrinal, material, ritual, mythological and experiential dimensions? What are they? Is it a religion?

- **Discuss, analyse and respond to** the place of humanism in relation to world religions in an essay. A possible title: 'Pressure group or religious alternative: "Humanism in Britain is not really an alternative to religion. It's more like an anti-religious pressure group." How far do you agree that humanism is more like a pressure group than a religion?'

Section 4   Resources

Resourcing RE: A broad approach

What makes a good resource?

There is seldom enough money for resources in schools and teachers are ingenious in matching limited funds to unlimited needs.

This overview comments on some of the essentials or desirables for RE, and suggests that a balance between different types of resource is best for good learning.

People

The first two resources available in RE are the **teachers** and the **pupils**.

As RE is centrally concerned with shared human experience, and with a personal search for meaning, it is important that the classroom atmosphere of an RE lesson should enable pupils to feel confident about sharing their own experience, ideas and perspectives. It is appropriate that pupils should be able to bring to the enquiry the riches of their own family culture and their personal insights.

Books

The mainstay of much work in RE remains the textbook. A vast range is on offer, and teachers need to use inspection copy services to agree where to invest most wisely. Whatever sections of the syllabus, or age groups, are involved, the following four criteria will guide the choice:

- **Integrity**. Is it clear that books have integrity in terms of the religions they address? For example, do books about Hinduism have consultants or authors who are Hindus?

- **Engagement and challenge**. Are the books engaging and challenging for the age group? For example, are the books more than merely factual, inviting engagement with issues and perspectives? Do teaching points arise from the use of good quality photographs, diagrams, drawings and other illustrations? Are there aids to understanding?

- **Educational standpoint**. Are the books written from a clearly educational standpoint? For example, it is unsatisfactory to use books written for a church audience to teach Christianity in a mixed setting.

- **Value for money**. Do the books represent value for money, enabling many children to learn to their potential? Some books are well worth a place in the class library,

Visual resources

Videos, DVDs, posters, photo packs, photographs and digital images enable pupils to see for themselves aspects of the practice of religion from all over the world.

The internet can extend considerably the range of images which can be brought easily into the RE classroom. Also, the ready availability of digital cameras makes it easier than ever before for teachers and pupils to provide their own images.

Wherever an image is used, it should be used as a **resource in its own right**, and not purely for decorative effect.

- **Responding to images**. In response to an image, pupils could be asked to respond to questions such as the following:

  - What do you notice?

  - What is happening and who is involved?

  - What do you think will happen next?

  - What emotions are being shown?

  - How does the image make you feel?

  - What does the creator/artist want to say?

  - What questions would you like to ask the creator/artist? How might s/he reply?

  - What religious questions is this image trying to comment on?

  - What have you learned from considering this image?

Artefacts

Religious artefacts in the classroom are a valuable way of adding authenticity and interest to the RE curriculum.

Collections of artefacts can be made available to schools in a variety of ways:

- school budget for RE
- loan services (LA or other)
- sharing between schools
- donations from local faith communities.

However artefacts are made available, they can enrich learning when used as a window into the community which produced them.

Visitors

Visits to school by members of a faith community are also powerful opportunities for RE. In an increasingly secular society many young people have little experience of engaging in dialogue with those who seek to live out a religious commitment.

Good practice when bringing religious visitors into school includes:

- **Assessing the suitability** of a visitor for the purpose you have in mind. Ideally meet the person yourself beforehand, or seek recommendation from a reliable teacher in another school.

- **Preparing well in advance** so that the visit is a natural and purposeful part of the programme of study.

- **Informing parents and governors** about the nature and purpose of the visit, who the visitor is and what they represent.

- **Briefing the visitor** on the ethos, aims and policies of the school, and the aspect of the RE curriculum to which they are contributing. Clarify the length and type of their input, any equipment they might need, and practicalities such as directions to the school.

- **Discussing the types of teaching and learning methods** which will engage pupils in view of their age and ability.

- **Debriefing lesson with the visitor,** so that there is opportunity to reflect on what went well, and make changes if appropriate. This is also an opportunity to say thank you.

Visits

A highlight of any RE programme is often the trip to a church, synagogue, mandir, mosque or other place of worship. This means hard work for the teacher, but the reward is that pupils have a genuine experience of the place, and the community that has created it.

Good visits have the following characteristics:

- they **build positive attitudes**
- they are **sensitively planned**
- the **build on preparatory work**
- they are **interesting and active**
- they are **integrated with a programme of study.**

A range of **'virtual visits'** can be found on the internet, and also on CD/DVD. Although these can never be as good as the 'real thing', they do have a valuable role within the RE curriculum. They can:

- **provide access** to places it is not possible to visit, e.g. Makkah

- **facilitate preparation and follow-up work** for visits or visitors

- **support research and revision**, as they can be 're-visited'.

What the pupils say:

'You didn't get the "feel" of a real church.'

'A real visit would show you more and you would understand it because you've seen it.'

'You can touch it and look closely at the colours in a real church. You can't look really closely in the virtual visit.'

'You couldn't see all of the church – you can only see what they chose to put there.'

'There were no real people praying at these.

It was bare.'

'It is more inspiring than a real church.'

Stories, poems and sacred texts

Providing opportunities for pupils to engage with a variety of texts important to religious traditions and faith communities is an integral part of the RE curriculum.

Select texts according to:

- the requirements of your syllabus or trust deed
- the reading age and ability of your pupils.

Plan the use of selected texts:

- with a clear idea of learning outcomes (what do you want your pupils to know, understand and be able to do as a result of their encounter with the story or text?)
- ensuring variety of type, religion and method of presentation across a key stage
- valuing and respecting the integrity of pupils assuming neither a faith position nor prior knowledge.

Use a variety of ways of telling and working with religious texts or stories:

- **traditional resources** (e.g. watch and listen to video and audio versions, or use the teacher as storyteller)
- **online sacred texts** (e.g. www.biblegateway.com and www.sacred-texts.com)
- **visitors** (e.g. invite a local member of the faith being studied into the classroom to tell the story and explain what it means to them)
- **creative writing** (e.g. provide opportunities for pupils to express meaning, questions and personal reflection in the form of prose, poetry, diary entry, newspaper report, letter, script)
- **creative arts** (e.g. provide opportunities for pupils to explore and express their understanding using drama, role-play, freeze-frame, dance, choral speaking, guided visualisation, cartoon drawing, art, audio and video recording)
- **reading pictures** (e.g. responding to a visual representation of a story, working out what is happening in the picture and speculating about what may have happened before, and what might happen next).

Reviews and evaluations

Evaluating resources is necessary but time-consuming. **Printed** and **online** reviews of RE resources reviewed by teachers, sometimes with suggestions for classroom use, are available.

Online message boards for RE teachers are also helpful, as you can ask a specific question, relating to your own context/phase.

Reviews

- **RE Today Services** (termly subscription mailing) www.retoday.org.uk
- **REOnline** www.reonline.org.uk
- **Schoolzone** www.schoolzone.co.uk
- **TEEM** www.teem.org.uk
- **Teachers TV** www.teachers.tv
- **Curriculum Online** www.curriculumonline.gov.uk

Online message boards

- **TES staffroom** www.tes.co.uk
- **Becta Schools** http://schools.becta.org.uk
- **Yahoo Groups: Teachers** http://groups.yahoo.com/group/RE-teachers.

Copyright

The copyright associated with all resources used in the classroom should be in line with legal requirements and LA policy.

Information relating to text and electronic materials is available from **The Copyright Licensing Agency (CLA)**, Saffron House, 6–10 Kirby Street, London EC1N 8TS or at www.cla.co.uk.

Information relating to electronic materials is available from

Becta, Millburn Hill Road, Science Park, Coventry, CV4 7JJ http://schools.becta.org.uk.